DRAWING THE LINE

Drawing the Line

PAUL GOODMAN

 *Random House : New York*

FIRST PRINTING

Copyright, 1946, © 1962, by Paul Goodman
All rights reserved under International and Pan-American Copyright
Conventions. Published in New York by Random House, Inc., and
simultaneously in Toronto, Canada, by Random House of Canada, Limited.
Manufactured in the United States of America
by H. Wolff, New York
Designed by Marshall Lee
Library of Congress catalog card number: 62–21464

This book is for Sally

Preface

Young friends have asked me to republish the out-of-print *May Pamphlet* of 1945. They say it makes more sense today than when I wrote it. Since that date our organized style of society, which I then called *Sociolatry* after Auguste Comte, has yearly become more relentless, and young people need more encouragement to resist it. My useful idea seems to be that it is self-betrayal on some concrete issue, that inwardly one knows to be crucial, that breaks the spirit and destroys integrity. (Young people who have not yet performed any works have to be very jealous of their integrity.)

Also, since that date, alas, the endless drizzle of the Cold War has made my kind of anarchist-pacifism unhappily endlessly relevant to another generation, to their peace actions and their personal decisions. The *May Pamphlet* was written before the Cold War "began," say, in 1947, and I might be dismayed at what a good prophet I have proved to be on the essential connection between our system of society and the Cold War. But I was only reading off, like many others, the causes plain to see. The Cold War did not "begin" in 1947, it was there. We had the Cold War before the Bomb. As I grimly predicted in *The State of Nature* (in 1944), "This time the Duration will last longer than the war."

In any case, here we are now. I, like you, have to cope intellectually, and physically, with 1962. Now we have also the Bomb. So in reprinting the earlier "prediction," I have included with it the pieces that I have been writing in response to recent facts.

The two parts of this little book, "Spring 1945" and "Winter 1962," have an identical philosophical and political position. This might mean simply that I am a stubborn fool who has not learned anything in seventeen years. I am afraid it means, rather, that there is really nothing else to say. Our society has not developed any new charms or exits. We must still look at it this hard way, and try to live, if we are to live at all, in our own community. We still believe that War is not discussable as a policy—it is already a betrayal of sanity to discuss it. Those who are expert in game-theory will find nothing for them here.

Yet there is a big difference in the tone of the two parts of this book. The difference is in me. I wrote the *May Pamphlet* for myself. I was having a disagreement with the Selective Service and was set to go to jail, though this was entirely against both my prudent principles and my wishes. (My philosophical and political position was Dodging. Fortunately, the United States and I came to an accommodation.) So these earlier meditations have a passionate syntax, which is again, perhaps, why they speak to disgusted young people today. (I notice also the melancholy fact that seventeen years ago I used more sexual illustrations than I do now.)

Since that time, however, I have become a "well-known author." The pieces of 1962 were prepared on demand, for public occasions, and naturally I now speak about the Establishment on more intimate acquaintance. The essay on the Administration was written because *Dissent* sent me to Washington to report. The "Remarks on War Spirit" were written for a conference of experts called by Professor Melman at Columbia. "On the Worldwide General Strike for Peace" was a speech at a rally at the Community Church on the first night of our first strike. "The Ineffectuality of Some Intelligent People" is made of two sermons, one to the Unitarians of Cleveland on their centennial, the other to the New York Committee of Correspondence for the radio. And the little meditation "For Tom" pretty much tells how I feel about such occasions. I am tired.

Despite the alleged temptations, I do not find that being a well-known author and being called on for public speeches has reconciled me to the American way of life. Our Establishment does not improve on closer acquaintance. One advantage of being a "success" is that I can now say my say without being accused of sour grapes. Indeed, the main thing that I have to teach my young friends is not the doctrine of Drawing the Line, but the perhaps encouraging, and certainly painful, factual demonstration that a man can hold such a doctrine and more or less live it during years of vicissitudes, and be still pitching. It is not impossible to "make it," to be somewhat accepted by the great world; but if you are still conscious, you will be stricken with the same dismay.

As I write this, they are testing their atom bombs again. And we, of course, are trying to stop them the best we know how.

The hope in face-to-face community that I have expressed in this book is still the only truth I know. But to make community work, people must be practical. Unfortunately—I suppose inevitably—most of the younger people drawn to these ideas are unbelievably inept; they are hung up, they break down; they do not know how to cope. They are honest and courageous— they do not have the fatal handicaps of prejudice, puritanism, or status seeking—but as if paying a penalty for this much freedom, they seem to be unable to carry through the simplest household plan. Visiting them does not give one many cheerful hours. The way to live is obvious because it is elementary; but we have gotten so complicated that it is just this that makes it hard.

April, 1962
New York City

Contents

SPRING 1945
The May Pamphlet

1

On treason against natural societies

We speak of Society, with a capital S, as "against the interests of Society," as though it were a unitary thing, more than the loose confederation of lesser societies which also admittedly exist. The unanimity of behavior in the industrial, economic, military, educational, and mass-entertained Society certainly justifies the usage. Some philosophers call Society "inorganic," meaning that many of the mores, e.g., traffic congestion, are too remote from biological functions and impede them. But in the classical sense of organism, namely that the least parts mutually cause each other, our Society is more organic than societies have ever been; every action, especially the absurd ones, can be shown to have social causes and to be a social necessity. Disease is no less organic than health.

Yet in some of the strongest meanings of social unity, Society is almost chaotic. One such is the confusion of moral judgments in the most important personal issues. Thus, ought a girl to be a virgin at marriage? Is there a single standard for husband and wife? Is theft within the law permissible? Is patriotism ridiculous? It would be possible to collect millions of votes on either side of such questions. I have made a practice of asking various persons what would be their attitude to receiving an incestuous brother and sister as overnight guests, and on this issue got many diverse replies.

Of course the universal confusion and toleration in such matters is itself a sign of social unanimity: namely, that people have agreed to divorce (and disregard) intimate personal concerns and opinions from the public ritual that exerts social pressure. The resulting uniformity of dress, behavior, desire is at the same time intense and bloodless; and there is no longer such a thing as earnest speech.

Now with regard to the legal penalty for crimes, like theft, bigamy, addiction, treason, murder, no such confusion and toleration exists. Once the case is brought to court, there is little diversity of judgment and punishment. One is appalled at the wooden morality that one meets in courts. Yet obviously the lack of social pressure keeps many cases out of court, for there is no scandal; adultery, for example, is a crime that is never brought to court. Does not this put the criminal law in an extraordinary position, and reduce the work of juries—which ought to express the strength of social opinion—to the merely logical function of judging evidence, which a judge could do better?

But the discrepancy between the moral and legal judgment of crime is deeply revealing. On the one hand the people, distracted by their timetable and their commodities, are increasingly less disturbed by the passional temptations that lead to crime; these are condoned, sophisticatedly understood rather than felt, partially abreacted by press and movies; they do not seem diabolic; the easy toleration of the idea goes with trivializing the wish. But on the other hand, the brute existence of any society whatever always in fact depends on the personal behavior of each soul; and a coercive society depends on instinctual repression. Therefore the Law is inflexible and unsophisticated. It is as though *Society knows the repressions that make its existence possible, but to the members of Society this knowledge has become unconscious. In this way is achieved the maximum of coercion by the easiest means.* The separation of personal and political and of moral and legal is a sign that to be coerced has become second nature. Thus it is that people are "protected from the cradle to the grave"!

Many (I believe most) of the so-called crimes are really free acts whose repression causes our timidity; natural society has a far shorter list of crimes. But on the contrary, *there is now an important class of acts that are really crimes and yet are judged indifferent or with approval by law and morals both. Acts which lead to unconcerned behavior are crimes. The separation of natural concern and institutional behavior is not only the sign of coercion, but is positively destructive of natural societies.* Let me give an obvious example.

Describing a bombed area and a horror hospital in Germany, a sergeant writes: "In modern war there are crimes not criminals. In modern society there is evil but there is no devil. Murder has been mechanized and rendered impersonal. The foul deed of bloody hands belongs to a bygone era when man could commit his own sins. . . . Here, as in many cases, the guilt belonged to the machine. Somewhere in the apparatus of bureaucracy, memoranda, and clean efficient directives, a crime has been committed." These have become familiar observations: the lofty bombardier is not a killer, just as the capitalist trapped in the market does not willingly deal slow death, etc. The system and now the machine itself! are guilty. Shall we bring into court the tri-motor airplane?

The most blessed thing in the world is to live by faith without imputation of guilt: having the Kingdom within. Lo, these persons have no imputation of guilt, and have they the Kingdom within?—riders, as Hawthorne said, of the Celestial Railway!

The crime that these persons—we all in our degree—are committing happens to be the most heinous in jurisprudence: it is a crime worse than murder. It is Treason. Treason against our natural societies so far as they exist.

Not all commit Treason to our natural societies in the same degree; some are more the principals, some more the accomplices. But it is ridiculous to say that the crime cannot be imputed or that any one commits it without intent and in ignorance. For every one knows moments in which he conforms against his nature, in which he suppresses his best spontaneous impulse, and cowardly takes leave of his heart. The steps which he takes to habituation and unconsciousness are crimes which entail every subsequent evil of enslavement and mass murder. The murder cannot be directly imputed, the sergeant is right; but the continuing treason must be imputed. (Why is he *still* a sergeant?)

Let us look a little at the horrible working out of this principle of imputation, which must nevertheless be declared just. We are bred into a society of mixed coercion and nature. The strongest natural influences—parental concern, childish imitation; adolescent desire to stand among one's brothers and be independent; an artisan's ability to produce something and a citizen's duty—all of these are unnaturally exerted to make us renounce and forget our natures. We conform to institutions that up to a certain point give great natural satisfactions, food, learning, and fellowship—then suddenly we find that terrible crimes are committed and we are somehow the agents. And some of us can even remember when it was that we compromised, were unwisely prudent, dismissed to another time a deeper satisfaction than convenient, and obeyed against our better judgment.

It is said the system is guilty, but the system is its members coerced into the system. It is also true that the system itself exercises the coercion.

Thus: a man works in a vast factory with an elaborate division of labor. He performs a repetitive operation in itself senseless. Naturally this work is irksome and he has many impulses to "go fishing," not to get up when the alarm clock rings, to find a more interesting job, to join with some other machinists in starting a small machine shop and try out certain ideas, to live in the country, etc. But against these impulses he meets in the factory itself and from his fellow workers (quite apart from home pressures) the following plausible arguments: that they must band together in that factory and as that factory, and in that industry and as that industry, to fight for "better working conditions," which mean more pay, shorter hours, fringe benefits; and the more militant organizers used even to demonstrate that by this means they could ultimately get control of all industry and smash the profit system.

None of this quite answers the original irk of the work itself; but good! A workman commits himself to this program. Now, however, since no one has native wit enough to decide for a vast factory and industry, and all industry, what to demand and when to demand it, and what means are effective, our man must look to others for direction concerning his own felt dissatisfaction. He fights for more pay when perhaps he does not primarily care about improving his standard of living but wants to accomplish something of his own between the cradle and the grave; he fights for seniority, when in fact he does not want the job, etc., etc. The issues of the fight are now determined by vast, distant forces; the union itself is a vast structure and it is tied to the whole existing Society. Next he finds that he is committed not to strike at all, but to help manufacture machines of war. The machines are then "guilty"!

True, the impulses of such a man are vague, romantic, and what is called adolescent; even if realizable they would not lead to full satisfaction. Nevertheless their essence is deep and natural. A program is a crime that does not meet the essence of the industrial irk, the unsatisfactory job, but shunts across it. The worker who does a job by coercion (e.g., to eat) is a traitor. When he is sidetracked into a good but irrelevant program, he is a traitor.

I have chosen a hard example that will rouse opposition. Let me choose a harder that will rouse even more.

A very young adolescent, as is usual enough, has sexual relations with his playfellows, partly satisfying their dreams of the girls, partly drawing on true homosexual desires that go back to earlier narcissism and mother-identifications of childhood. But because of what they have been taught in their parochial school and the common words of insult whose meaning they now first grasp, all these boys are ashamed of their acts; their pleasures are suppressed and in their stead appear fist fights and violence. The youth grows up, soon marries. Now there is conscription for a far-off war, whose issues are dubious and certainly not part of his immediate awareness and reaction. But his natural desire to oppose the conscription is met by the strong attractiveness of getting away from the wife he is a little tired of, back to the free company of the boys in camp; away from the fatherly role of too great responsibility, back to the dependence on a paternal sergeant. The camp life, drawing always on a repressed but finally thinly disguised sexuality, cements the strongest bonds of fellowship amongst the soldiers. Yet any overt sexual satisfaction among them is out of the question. Instead the pairs of buddies pick up prostitutes together, copulate with them in the same room, and exchange boasts of prowess. Next this violent homosexuality, so near the surface but always repressed and thereby gathering tension, turns into a violent sadism against the enemy: it is all knives and guns and bayonets, and raining bombs on towns, and driving home one's lust in the guise of anger to f——— the Japs.*

It is a hard thing to impute the crime of treason against natural society to these men who do not even consciously know what their impulse is. They know as boys; shall we blame boys? And even the adults, priests, and teachers who invidiously prevent the boys' antics do it out of unconscious envy and resentment. But they at least could know better, or why are they teachers?

It is horrifying, though not useless, thus to impute treason to the particular persons and to trace the institutional crimes, which are but symptoms and results, back to the incidents of coercion and resignation. The guilty ones turn out to be little children and dear parents, earnest radicals, teachers unconscious of their intent, and even ancestors who are dead. Thank God we do not need to think of punishments, for we know—following Socrates of old— that the punishment of injustice is to be what one is. The persons who separate themselves from nature have to live every minute of their lives without the power, joy, and freedom of nature. And we, who apparently suffer grave sanctions from such persons, betray on our faces that we are drawing on forces of nature.

But in fact the case is like the distinction in theology between the Old Law and the New. In the Old Law all are guilty, in the New they may easily be saved. We see that in fact everybody who still has life and energy is continually manifesting some natural force and is today facing an unnatural coercion. And now, in some apparently trivial issue that nevertheless is a key, he *draws the line!* The next step for him to take is not obscure or difficult, it

---

* The next generation of these pent-up young men are practicing *karate*, borrowed from, as if inevitably, the same Japanese.

presents itself at once; it is even forcibly presented by Society! Modern society does not let one be—it is too total—it forces one's hand.

May, 1945.

2

Reflections on drawing the line

i.

A free society cannot be the substitution of a "new order" for the old order; it is the extension of spheres of free action until they make up most of the social life. (That such liberation is step by step does not mean that it can occur without revolutionary disruption, for in many spheres—e.g., war, economics, sexual education—any genuine liberation whatsoever involves a total change.)

In any present society, though much and even an increasing amount is coercive, nevertheless much is also free. If it were not so, it would be impossible for a conscientious libertarian to co-operate or live there at all; but in fact we are constantly drawing the line beyond which we refuse to co-operate. In creative work, in passion and sentiment, in spontaneous recreation, there are healthy spheres of nature and freedom: it is the spirit of these that we most often extrapolate to all acts of utopian free society, to making a living, to civil life and law. But indeed, even the most corrupt and coercive functions of the present society draw on good natural power—the pity of it—otherwise the society could not survive for one moment; for free natural power is the only source of existence. Thus, people are fed, though the means, the cost, and the productive relations are coercive; and the total war would be the end of us all were it not for the bravery and endurance of mankind.

Free action is to live in present society as though it were a natural society. This maxim has three consequences, three moments:

(1) In the spheres which are in fact free and natural, we exercise personal excellence and give mutual aid.

(2) In many spheres which seem to be uncoerced, we have nevertheless been trapped into unnatural ways by the coercion that has formed us; for example, we have become habituated to the American timetable and the standard of living, though these are unnatural and coercive through and through. Here the maxim demands that we first correct ourselves.

(3) Finally, there are those natural acts or abstentions which clash openly with the coercive laws: these are the "crimes" which it is beholden on a free man to commit, as his reasonable desire demands and as the occasion arises. (See below, "A Touchstone . . .")

The free spirit is rather millenarian than utopian. A man does not look forward to a future state of things which he tries to bring about by suspect means; but he draws now, so far as he can, on the natural force in him that is no different in kind from what it will be in a free society, except that there it will have more scope and be persistently reinforced by mutual aid and fraternal conflict. *Merely by continuing to exist and act in nature and freedom, a free man wins the victory, establishes the society;* it is not necessary for him to be the victor *over* any one. When he creates, he wins; when he corrects his prejudices and habits he wins; when he resists and suffers, he wins. I say it this way in order to tell honest persons not to despond when it seems that their earnest and honest work is without "influence." The free man does not seek to influence groups but to act in the natural groups essential to him—for most human action is the action of groups. Consider if a million persons, quite apart from any "political" intention, did only natural work and did the best they could. The system of exploitation would disperse like fog in a hot wind. But of what use is the action, born of resentment, that is bent on correcting abuses yet never does a stroke of nature?

The action drawing on the most natural force will in fact establish itself. Might is right: but do not let the violent and the cowed imagine for a moment that their brutality is might. What great things have *they* accomplished, in practice, art, or theory? Their violence is fear hidden from themselves by conceit, and nothing comes from it.

ii.

Now I have been liberally using the terms "nature," "natural," and their contraries to attribute value and disvalue, as "natural and unnatural institutions." Do not these terms in this use lead to self-contradiction? for obviously the bad institutions as well as the good have come to be by natural process. A bad convention exists by natural causes; how are we to call it unnatural?

Let us consider the example of a language like English, and I want to distinguish three notions: physical and social nature, natural convention, and unnatural convention. It is physically and socially natural for people to speak: they have speech organs; they communicate with these; children express their feelings with determinate cries and imitate their parents' speech behavior. But any speech is some language or other. Speech organs, need to communicate, the expression of feelings, the desire to imitate and identify: these give the potentiality of speaking some language or other; historical circumstances make the language in fact English. It is usual to call the historical language conventional, but it is a "natural convention," in that the convention of English is a means of making the power of speech into a living act. Here we have the clue to how we can speak of an "unnatural convention": *an unnatural convention is one that prevents a human power from becoming a living act.* Thus, English is becoming unnatural because of its use in advertising. The technique of advertising is to establish an automatic reflex response, an immediate connection between certain words and the behavior of paying out money: thus it debauches the words so that they no longer express felt need, nor communicate a likeness of affection between persons, continuous with the imitation of parents and peers, nor correspond to the desire for objects really experienced. These functions of honest speech are shunted over by a successful advertisement. But these functions are the strongest and the creative power in speech. Therefore we can say that the abuse of English prevents the power of speech from becoming a living act; it is unnatural.

But it is objected that automatic response is also natural: it is physically and socially necessary for life, as consider the words "Look out!" or "Fire!" But let us patiently consider the order and ratio of such alarm words to the rest of speech. If they are too numerous, their emergency is blunted, just as indiscriminate profanity has no expletive force. What is the natural order of emergency and nonemergency situations, so that the strongest powers of health, safety, and pleasure may not be prevented from becoming living acts? The sense of emergency, natural in itself, still inhibits vegetation, memory, reflection. (It likewise inhibits, by the way, the religious, eschatological, sense of emergency.) Taken at face value, the techniques of advertising and automatic political slogans express a state of chronic alarm!

Yet to be sure, as we consider it deeper, this *is* the historical situation; there is nothing conventional about such techniques; and our poor English, like a faithful servant, is sacrificed to urgent need. The society that needs to buy up the products of its industry *is* in a state of chronic alarm: what time has it for vegetation, memory, reflection? And the "high" standard of living thus purchased exists in emergency conditions that are preventive of any natural standard of living whatever, for there is no vegetative pleasure and reflection, and no emptiness in which inventions can flower. In haste and alarm, hearing and buying, a man cannot get his bearings, he is swept along, falls into debt and is open to still further coercion. No one can even quit a job. But we do not need to go thus roundabout through the analysis of linguistic usage to know that our way of life is compulsive. We can see it by direct observation on the street.

People are both frightened and deadened. It is a poor kind of democracy in which nobody stands out instead of everybody standing out. (Instead there are, pathetically, "celebrities.") Those who constrain strong natural power are always themselves under constraint. The prison guard is himself in jail, yes even the Warden.

But in any great collaboration, in art or theory or practice, the signature of each collaborator is apparent in the outcome. The plaid has the bright color of its threads.

iii.

What is natural coercion and what is unnatural coercion? I doubt that I can answer this hard question to my own satisfaction, but sufficiently for the gross facts that we are concerned with. Education has always elements of natural coercion, but government by state or society is unnatural.

Natural coercion seems to go with natural dependency. An infant is dependent, he is part of his mother's field. A growing child is more voluntarily dependent; he is secure in the grownups' care and attention, and he grows in independence partly by imitation and partly by withdrawal from those in whom he is secure. A child grows teeth as he ceases to suckle, and he begins to walk when he is big enough to begin to walk away—*into* independence, for it is something positive. Yet coercion and violence inevitably occur, for the child grows in the predetermined culture of the adults and among the anger of the adults being themselves. To a child this must seem like any other reality—the part that doesn't make sense—but intensely interesting. At least he learns to keep out of the way. (In my opinion this is all he learns, for beautiful new truths are not communicated by a clout on the head.)

A pupil depends on a teacher who exercises authority and sets up the lessons. There is probably more of this than is necessary, but again the progress of the pupil and the aim of the teacher is the independence of the pupil from the teacher. If a person has maintained his trust through the previous storms of life, he can learn from teachers. A person who cannot surrender to archaic attitudes of dependency is probably not truly docile. But if previous childish dependency has been too frightened or cowed, a young person both will not trust his teachers and cannot grow to become their peer. He is prevented from drawing on the knowledge and power embodied in them. By this sign, therefore, we can say that the parental coercion was violent and unnatural.

The discouragement of childish sexuality leads to later anxiety; toilet training leads to "ruliness"; etc. So these must be called unnatural coercion. In general, when strong drives are frustrated and punished and a child begins to inhibit himself, to fill the vacuum of his life he identifies with precisely those who frustrate him: they are wise, they are authorities. The child has now lost both his desires and his power of initiation.

What is unique about human nature, however, is its *long* dependency. This is a great opportunity, for education, but it has also proved to be a great disaster. To the child, it seems to me, the danger is not generally that his ego will fail to crystallize, a case of psychosis, but that it will crystallize too rapidly, in too closed a system, against the inner and outer world from which in the end we must draw the forces of life. This has been especially noted with regard to the sexual drives, against which the ego sets itself, becoming erotized in turn—for when you can't love anything else you have to love yourself. But not enough has been said about the uncanny ignorance, stupidity, incuriosity, lack of perception and observation that characterize us, and which must also be attributed to inhibition by the too narrow, shut-in, and conceited ego. And so we fall into the opposite disaster, that the grownups have never learned to cope with the environment. They are dependent on governments.

Education is the furnishing by adults of imitable patterns of interpretation and attitude, *not* to train the child, but on the contrary so that the child, by relying on them and trying them, can take his time and not have to stand too quickly alone as sole authority. Adults provide and decide where children cannot yet provide and decide. This is coercion, always partly corporal, putting the child in the way of experience and out of the way of automobiles and poison. We can define natural coercion as a knowledgeable decision that preserves for the child his greatest inner and outer power to work up into experience and art.

But I do not think there is any use of docility to government, for it has not much to teach. Of the simple goods, food, shelter, safety, over which great constituted bodies like governments and economic systems claim authority, there is not a single one that the average adult person ought not to be competent to decide about. Every one knows he is hungry and wants food, or knows enough to come in out of the rain. If he has not developed to this point, it is that he has been maimed by unnatural coercion. But it is the way of authority to maim initiative and then prove that people have no initiative, and to pre-empt the means of livelihood and then show that people do not have the means to cope. There is plenty of rhetoric, and the use of force, to persuade people to continue as we do; but there is absolutely no public discussion and reasoning to consider whether the way we do *anything*—produce goods, run the schools, communicate ideas, elect officers—is the most efficient and sensible. Yet this is supposed to be an experimenting animal.

At present, of course, almost every man considers himself incompetent to provide the simplest goods. The state and other established institutions do decide for him. People are stupefied largely because they have so few interesting problems to work on; and finally they cannot decide whether they are cold, hurt, lonely, or even bored. They are not sure of anything. They are in a chronic state of alarm. Under these circumstances, orators easily pose as fathers and leaders. And this is called progressive, it is a New Deal. The "conservatives," on the other hand, want to stay with the oppressions of 1910 or perhaps Prince Metternich. It is only the anarchists who are really conservative, for they want to conserve sun and space, animal nature, primary community, experimenting inquiry.

iv.

A man is dependent on his mother Earth. We are forever dependent in the universe, but not on princes.

It is false that social relationships are primarily interpersonal. The strongest bonds in natural groups are continuous with passions and impulses previous to the organization of the egos of the members. These are love and fraternity. How different is the ju-

ridical equality of the social psychologists of "interpersonal relationships" from the creative unanimity and rivalry of revolutionary fraternity! Brothers vie to excel individually, but catching
fire from each other they achieve what none of them had it in him
to do alone.

It is not our social nature to go it alone. It does not follow that
one must conform to Society. It is enough to find-and-make a
band, two hundred, of the like-minded, to know that oneself is
sane though the rest of the city is batty.

The free man manifests the nature in him much more vehemently than we who have been trained to uniformity. His voice,
gestures, and countenance express the great range of experience
from child to sage. When he hears the hypocrite orator use words
that arouse disgust, he vomits in the crowd.

We can conceive of a man whose ego takes far longer to crystallize than ours; whose ego still is forming out of vast systems of
inner and outer experience, and works with forces beyond those
that we have settled for. Such a vast ego belongs to Christ or
Buddha; we may confidently predict that it will perform miracles.
To him they are matter-of-fact.

In the mixed society of coercion and nature, our characteristic
act is Drawing the Line, beyond which we cannot co-operate. All
the heart-searching and purgatorial anxiety concerns this question,
Where to draw the line? I'll say it bluntly: the anxiety goes far
beyond reason. Since the extreme positions are clear black and
white, and they exist plain to suffer and enjoy, and since it can
be shown that one step leads to another in either direction: in the
in-between murk *any* apparently arbitrary line is good enough.
And one's potential friends among the people, to whom one wants
to set an example, are moved by the challenging action, not the
little details of consistency.

No particular drawn line will ever be defensible logically. But
the right way from any line will prove itself more clearly step by
step and blow by blow.

Yet to each person it seems to make all the difference where he
draws the line! This is because just these details are the symbolic
key to his repressed powers—and with each repression, guilt for
the acceptance of it. Thus one man will speak in their court but

will not pay a tax; another will write a letter but will not move his feet; another is nauseated by innocent bread and fasts. Why are the drawn lines so odd and logically inconsistent? why are they maintained with such irrational stubbornness—precisely by free people who are usually so amiable and easy-smiling? The actions of nature are by no means inconsistent; they are sequences of even rather simple causes; following the probabilities does not lead one astray but to see one's way more clearly. But the fact is that each of us has been unconsciously coerced by our training and acceptance; the inner conflicts now begin to appear, in the inconsistency of drawing the line, and all the fear, guilt, and rage. Let us draw our lines and have this out!

A free man would have no such problems; he would not have finally to draw a line in their absurd conditions which he has disdained from the very beginning. The truth is that he would regard coercive sanctions as no different from the other destructive forces of brute nature, to be prudently avoided.

A free man, so long as he creates and goes by his clear and distinct ideas, can easily maintain in his soul many apparent contradictions; he is sure they will iron out; a loose system is the best system. But woe if at the same time he is persuaded into prejudices and coerced into conforming: then one day he will have the agony of drawing the line.

Well! there is a boyish joke I like to tell. Tom says to Jerry: "Do you want to fight? Cross that line!" and Jerry does. "Now," cries Tom, "you're on *my* side!"

We draw the line in their conditions; we proceed on our conditions.

May, 1945.

3

A touchstone for the libertarian program

The "political" program of libertarians is usually negative, for positive goods are achieved by other forces than (coercive) political institutions. But a program of opposition varies with the oppressions and restrictions. Libertarians must not fall into the trap of wasting force by still opposing what authority no longer proposes, while failing to see new kinds of exploitation. The mass press and radio of the democracies are masters at stealing liberal thunder; what are the words and acts that can expose this verbiage, which is often indeed well meant? Thus, industrial authority does not exercise the same forms of oppression when there is a technology of surplus as it used when there was a technology of scarcity. In scarcity, the chief means of profit for the exploiters consisted in the depression of the workers' standard of living to reproductive subsistence; in surplus, the problem is sometimes rather to compel and control an artificial "high" standard of living that will clear the shelves. This is again pure authoritarian compulsion, but exercised especially by psychological means, advertising, miseducation, and rousing the spirit of emulation. The result is that men insensibly find themselves even more enslaved in their time, choice, invention, spontaneity, and culture than in the black days of want, when at least a man's misery was uncontaminated and might produce a natural reaction. Given a surplus of goods and mass media of misinformation, it is possible for authority to cushion all crises and allow "freedom of expression" (or even encourage it as a safety valve) to a small eccentric press.

I should like to suggest a kind of touchstone for the right libertarian program in a period like the present when the corporate integration of the economy, morals, tastes, and information of the society is so tight: I mean when the press, the movies, etc., themselves commodities, generate an increasing flow of commodities. The touchstone is this: *does our program involve a large number of precisely those acts and words for which persons are in fact thrown into jail?* We must proceed on the assumption that the coercive society knows well which acts are a threat to it and which are not; acts which in fact rouse a coercive reaction have libertarian force; those which, though once coerced, are now tolerated, are likely to be stolen thunder that is not neutral but in fact coercive in its effects. Thus, it is no longer the case that the man who publicly speaks for the organized bargaining power of labor is jailed; on the contrary, he is approved. But this is not merely because organized labor has grown so strong as to compel its toleration (if it were this strong it could compel much more). It is because the organization of labor is a means of social control; higher wages are a means of profit—especially when by price controls the public market is becoming a company store; and it is increasingly convenient for labor to regard itself as a participant in the general corporation of production and consumption. On the contrary, the man who advocates a wildcat strike is thrown into jail, but not merely because the demands are dangerous to profits, but that he disrupts the ordered system, the due process. Again: the man who advocates (advertises or displays) moral vices that fit well into the commodity system is an agent of society; but the man who advocates (exemplifies) pleasures outside the system of exchange or that undermine the social discipline, is frowned on and jailed—thus, one may not steal, copulate in the park, or encourage the sexuality of children.

Concerning the "crimes" that are actually punished, a free man must ask himself: which of these are detrimental to any society, including even a more natural noncoercive society in which discipline is somewhat but not so deeply and widely grounded in (reasonable) successful repression and deliberate inhibition; which "crimes," on the contrary, are precisely the acts that would undermine the present coercive structure? I think that the list of the former would be small indeed—an obvious instance is murder. (Let me recommend William Morris' *News from Nowhere.*) But with regard to the latter, many beautiful opportunities could be found for libertarian action. What I urge is not that the libertarian at once bestir himself to commit such "crimes"—I do not think, by the way, that our small numbers would inconveniently crowd the jails; but that he proceed to loosen his own "discipline" and prejudice against these acts. For most of us do not realize how broadly and deeply the coercive relations in which we have been born and bred have disciplined us to the continuation of these coercive relations. Once his judgment is freed, then with regard to such "crimes" the libertarian must act as he should in every case whatsoever: if something seems true to his nature, important and necessary for himself and his fellows at the present moment, let him do it with moral good will and joy. Let him avoid the coercive consequences with natural prudence, not by frustation and timid denial of what is the case; for our acts of liberty are our strongest propaganda. Unfortunately, as people are, anxious and vulnerable, the immediate effect of an exercise of free power may be disturbing and sometimes disastrous—e.g., the schoolgirl who commits suicide because her roommate has sex with a boy friend. Certainly one must temper the wind to the shorn lamb, till she grows a fleece. But we must also calculate the long-range and universal effects of the spite, sadism, coldness, timidity that are produced by our present ways: how the boy who was always "such a good boy" blows up anyway and shoots his mother and father and four neighbors.

It is often cited as an example of the barbarity of America that here no distinction is made between "political prisoners" and "common criminals," that the political prisoner is degraded to the level of the criminal; yet in fact the "common criminal" has, although usually by the failure of repression and rarely by reason, probably committed a political crime.

Returning now to the starting point, the need to change the libertarian program with the change of the coercive circumstances, I should like to make a criticism of the continued use of one of the darling words of anarchist literature, the word "personal," as in "personal freedom," "personal expression," etc. The fact is that at present it is exactly the aim of all the organs of publicity, entertainment, and education so to form the personality that a man performs by his subjective personal choice just what is objectively advantageous for the coercive corporation, of which further he feels himself to be a part. Because of their use of the terms "free personality," "personal spontaneity," "personal participation," the hogwash of psychologists like Fromm and Horney has won the praise of even such an excellent anarchist as Herbert Read; yet it is not hard to show that their psychology has as its aim to produce a unanimity of spirit in the perfected form of the present social system, with its monster factories, streamlined satisfactions, and distant representative government. This kind of subjective personality is an effect of coercion, acting in the unconscious; it is not a causal principle of freedom. Going back to Rousseau, let me suggest the substitution of the word "natural," meaning those drives and forces, on both the animal and human level, which at present act themselves out in defiance of the conventions that we and our friends all agree to be outmoded and no longer "natural conventions," but which in a free society will be the motors of individual excellence and mutual aid.

To sum up: very many acts which are now called crimes are nature. It is often the very fact of treating natural acts as crimes that makes them become enormities, because of fear and the stupidity engendered by panic. Even libertarians acquiesce in these prejudices because their "free personalities" have been coercively formed and are subject to unconscious coercion. The internal repression of spontaneous natural forces is today more than ever, in our era of timetables and standardized pleasure, the chief means of dispiritment and coercion. Let us work to express not our "selves" but the nature in us. Let us not participate in coercive or merely conventional groups, symbols, and behavior. The freedom of the individual is the expression of the natural animal and social groups to which he in fact belongs. Re-examine the "crimes" which seem proper to yourself and see which are indeed not crimes but the natural behavior of natural groups.

A young woman friend was to appear in court (seeking custody of her child), and a dozen of us offered ourselves at her lawyer's office to be briefed as character witnesses. We were, in my opinion, sober and useful citizens; but when the lawyer questioned us, his face fell as he had to rule out one after another as entirely unpresentable. One excellent mother of three was not legally wed; a good father was known to be bisexual; an old friend was— a Negress; a brilliant and self-supporting man had no definable job; another looked like something the cat dragged in; another had been in and out of jail for various kinds of civil disobedience. It was hilarious—we stared at one another in dismay. It certainly wasn't our scene. But the question is, how many lively and productive persons could appear in that court, against a clever lawyer, without putting up a false front? I don't mean that Society as a whole is as unviable as a court of law, but it does pay to lie low. Yet if one lies low, how to make use of the social means and have sounding speech? There is the dilemma.

May, 1945

4

Natural violence

I have reached middle age and have not attended, nor even seen, a man dying or a baby being born. As things are arranged in our city, it is impossible to come close to a violent or noisome disease, unless professionally. What one meets in our city is a kind of health, usually mildly ailing, and a vigor youthful enough to ambulate. Decrepit age is confined to its rooms. One is faced with plenty of neurotics but rarely a maniac. In rural places there is as yet much more dying and being born socially, of both men and animals; but the tendency is not otherwise than with us. Again, the bourgeoisie (and my own class, the lumpen bourgeoisie) is more protected against such experience than the proletariat; but giant strides have been made toward extending protection to all. In general, women in childbirth necessarily are unprotected, but it is the practice to anodyze this experience as much as possible.

Men protect themselves from the major conditions of life. I do not say the major concerns, but surely the value of our concerns, such as they are, is problematical when they are not potentially, in ready memory and anticipation, related to their major conditions. Infants and children, it seems to me, are universally less protected; they have a closer acquaintance with their creature-anxiety, *Angst der Kreatur*. We others now successfully repress creature-anxiety from recall.

(Primitive people, of course, attempt to repress it, but they have not the means. In theory their art should therefore be more powerful than ours, and their neuroses, unless they have lucky institutions, more widespread. They are more alive than we and crazier than we.)

The facts of war revive the lost anxiety in a terrible way, but they are valueless for a natural culture. They are the breakdown of Society, but the exposed sufferer does not then have other feelings and habits to help him use these terrible truths for inventive life. The mentally broken soldiers who return from fiery fronts do not readjust to unnatural conventions, but they rarely create natural conventions—individual symptoms are not valuable social conventions—for the most part they are really ill as well as ill in the eyes of the community.

An example of childish invention comes to mind: One morning at our country school some men butchered a cow and strung it up and flayed it. It was the hour of recess for the smallest children and they ran and stood in a circle round the bloody sight and drank it in with lewd eyes, afterwards manifesting extreme fright, excitement, and nausea when meat was served them. But they invented a ritual game of flaying a cow, in which one of their number would put on a coat and the others strip it off.

Can we imagine a society that would have a better expression of its major conditions than ritual games?

I myself have been so disciplined that I cannot spontaneously and from my own experience see a way through our dilemma, yet it presents a crucial problem for us. Contrast the rational medical approach to birth, disease, decrepitude and death, with the rational efficient approach to industrial production. Wherever so-called efficiency in production leads to stultified and one-sided habits of the worker, we confidently say that the efficiency is inefficient in the long run because the means destroy the end. But medical efficiency—e.g., hospital technique or the therapeutic attitude—seems *prima facie* useful for our lives altogether, therefore for our full lives. On the other hand, the necessary isolation of the sick leads to a sterilization of general social experience that conceivably itself makes life flat and increases the flight into illness. It was better when illness was eerie, the province of the Asclepiads.

One is baffled and saddened by the spectacle of doctors straining their art to heal the soldiers hurt in the battle in which they themselves take part. They must, they are willing to heal the wounds of both sides at the same time as they fan the rage of one side. This is an heroic dedication, but there is something unnatural about it. Their medical training and practice have isolated some meanings from other meanings.

Certainly we others, unused to the primary facts of birth, life, and death, are easily coerced by the threat of them—we panic and are vulnerable to Terror—until the moment we recklessly plunge into disaster of our own making, and beyond what is necessary. We thus "control" it and avoid panic.

Strange as the phrase may seem, we must speak of "natural violence," just as previously we defined "natural coercion," although all violence is precisely the destruction, inhibition, or forcing of natural motions. *Natural violence is the destruction of habits or second natures in the interests of regaining the primary experiences of birth, infantile anxiety, grief and mourning for death, simple sexuality, etc.* I think this is the virtue of the "extreme situations" of the existentialists. Such natural violence can be demonstrated in many ordinary actions. An obvious example is the violence sought by and done to a virginal or sexually timid person who cannot, by character, will his or her own joy. The hand of the physician is gentle but is firm. Deeper than their fears, civilized people yearn for and welcome natural catastrophes like fires and hurricanes, that will strip them of their possessions and touch routine to the quick.

The "nonviolence" of doctrinal pacifists is unnatural and even somewhat wicked, unless it is, as Gandhi meant, a positive outpouring of love that burns away one's anger, and of understanding that gives light. To my mind, what generally passes for "nonviolence" is a spiteful stalling to exacerbate guilt. Anger is at least contactful; and it seems false not to let anger follow through and strike. It is interesting to see how usually, among reasonable people, the one blow, or the one exchange of blows, is the last; for it has re-established contact.

But so men also plunge recklessly into war, where there is no object to contact and there is no end to it. They rely on each other for mass hypnosis and social approval of their illusion, so they may keep striking with a good conscience. We must believe that they are not dreaming of their death, a psychological impossibility, but of putting the established ego in peril in order to bring it back into openness to the instincts. But the war destroys not only their conventions but their lives altogether; for those who survive, there is provided not new, more natural habits but social isolation and nervous breakdown; and for society as a whole, the war does not liberate natural associations and release social inventiveness, but on the contrary reinforces the coercive and authoritarian establishment. War is unnatural violence.

The people of the Middle Ages, as Huizinga has pointed out, lived in a welter of natural and unnatural violence. With us there is progressively less of natural violence; the unnatural violence is pent up until it bursts forth, as a great corporate institution, in these world wars.

In the state of nature no positive effect springs from a negative cause. Yet the free man is forever clearing the decks and seems to exert political pressure only by negation. This is natural violence. If he employs nonviolent "passive resistance," it is in order not to complicate further, by material weapons and authoritative organizations, the situation which is already too encumbered. He sets up the vacuum in our learned follies, so that original forces can operate to our advantage.

Resistance—patience—firmness—duty: these are not negative nor even passive virtues; they are not the restraint of force; they are action of the more elemental forces of primary nature; of time and clinging to one's place.

The anarchist apparently seeks to create a political vacuum; but it is the fertile vacuum of Tao, where heavy masses fall of their own weight and the invisible seeds germinate. He speaks a word that *heals* as it violates.

May-June, 1945.

5

Revolution, sociolatry, and war

i. *A Miscalculation in the Marxian Dynamics of Revolution*

According to Marx and Engels, the dynamism of the people's revolution into socialism rises from the interaction of two psychological attitudes: (a) the spiritual alienation of the proletariat, because of extreme division of labor and capitalist productive relations, from man's original concern with production and from natural social co-operation; (b) the brute reaction to intolerable deprivation brought on by the falling rate of profit and the capitalist crisis. To expand these points somewhat:

(a) To Marx and Engels the specific properties of humanity are the ability to produce things and to give mutual aid in production. But the subdivision of labor and the capitalist use of machine technology dehumanize production: a man makes only a part of a commodity sold on a distant market, and performing an automatic operation he employs only a modicum of his powers. Further, the conditions of bourgeois competition and wage slavery isolate men from each other and destroy mutuality, family life, comradeship. There is therefore nothing in the capitalist institutions to engage the deep interest or keep the loyalty of the proletariat. They are made into fractional people and these fractions of men are indifferent to the bourgeois mores and society.

(b) On the other hand they are not indifferent to starvation, disease, sexual deprivation, infant mortality, and death in war; but these are the results of the wage cuts, imperialism, unemployment, and fluctuation inherent in the bourgeois need to counteract the falling rate of profit and to reinvest. At the level of resentment and frustration and animal reaction to pain, there is concern for a violent change, there is latent rebellion.

From these attitudes, the revolutionary idea emerges somewhat as follows: driven by need to consult their safety, and with understanding given by usually middle-class teachers who explain the causes of their hurt, and with their original human aspirations recalled from forgetfulness and already fulfilled somewhat by comradely unity, the proletariat turns toward a new order, new foundations, a socialism immeasurably improved yet in its main features not unlike original human nature. By contrast to this idea, the life of the bourgeoisie itself seems worthless. And being increased in numbers and with their hands on the productive machinery of all society, the proletarians know that they can make the idea a reality.

Psychologically—and even anthropologically and ethically— this Marxian formula has great power, if indeed all its elements exist as prescribed. But on the contrary, if any of the elements are missing the formula is disastrous and takes us as far from fraternal socialism as can be. Now there is no question that point (b) is missing: that by and large over the last century in the advanced industrial countries the real wages of the working class as a whole have not lingered at the margin of *physical* subsistence and reproduction; they have advanced to a point where even revolutionary writers agitate for a "sociological standard of living." (The reasons, of course, are the astounding increase in productivity, the high rate of technical improvement, the need for domestic markets, and such gross profits that the rate of profit has lost paramount importance.) What has been the result?

The spiritual alienation of point (a) has gone even further, I suppose, than Marx envisaged. He followed the dehumanization of production to the last subdivision of labor into an automatic gesture, but I doubt whether he (being sane) could have foreseen that thousands of adult persons could work day in and day out and not know what they were making. He did not foresee the dehumanization of consumption in the universal domestic use of streamlined conveniences whose operation the consumer does not begin to understand; the destruction of even the free choices in the marketplace by mass advertising and monopolistic controls; the segregation among experts in hospitals of all primary experience of birth, pain, and death, etc., etc.

Yet now these fractional persons, alienated from their natures, are not brought sharply to look out for themselves by intolerable deprivation. On the contrary, they are even tricked, by the increase in commodities, into finding an imitation satisfaction in their "standard of living"; and the kind of psychological drive that moves them is—emulation! The demand of the organized proletariat for a living wage and tolerable working conditions, a demand that in the beginning was necessarily political and revolutionary in its consequences, now becomes a demand for a standard of living and for leisure to enjoy the goods, *accepting the mores of the dominant class.* (What are we to say of "leisure" as a good for an animal whose specific humanity is to be productive?) Then if these persons have gone over to the ideals of another class, it is foolish to call them any longer "proletarians" ("producers of offspring," as Marx nobly and bitterly characterized the workers); but given the apparently satisfied alienation from concern in production—and where do we see anything else?—it is also unjust to call them workers.

Marx saw wonderfully the emptiness of life in the modern system; but he failed to utter the warning that this emptiness could proceed so far that, without the spur of starvation, it could make a man satisfied to be a traitor to his original nature. What he relied on to be a dynamic motor of revolution has become the cause of treason.

Lastly, the scientific teachers of the masses are no longer concerned to recall us to our original creative natures, to destroy the inhuman subdivision of labor, to look to the bands of comrades for the initiation of direct action. On the contrary, their interest has become the health and smooth functioning of the industrial machine itself: they are economists of full employment, sociologists of belonging, psychologists of vocational guidance, and politicians of administrative bureaus.

So far the psychology of the masses. But in the psychology of the bourgeoisie there is a correlated difference from what Marx envisaged. The Marxian bourgeois has the following characteristics: (a) Preoccupied with exchange value, with money which is featureless, he is alienated from all natural personal or social interests; this makes all the easier his ruthless career of accumulation, reinvestment, exploitation, and war. (b) On the other hand, he embodies a fierce lust, real even though manic, for wealth and power. The conditions of his role are given by the economy, but he plays the role with all his heart; he is an individual, if not quite a man. The spur of a falling rate of profit or of closed markets, therefore, drives him on to desperate adventures.

By and large I do not think that this type is now very evident. Partly, to be sure, it is that the owning classes adopt a democratic camouflage for their protection; but the fact that they are willing to do this already shows that they are different men. Other factors seem to me important: (1) In absentee ownership there is an emasculation of the drive for maximum exploitation of the labor and the machine; the owner does not have the inspiration of his daily supervision; he is not approached by inventors and foremen, etc.; but the salaried manager is usually concerned with stability rather than change. (2) But even if the drive to improve the exploitation is strong, the individual capitalist is disheartened by the corporate structure in which most vast enterprises are now imbedded; he is embarrassed by prudent or timid confrères. (Government regulation is the last stage of this corporative timidity.) (3) Not least, it now seems that even in peacetime there is a limit to the falling rate of profit; technical improvement alone guarantees an annual increment of more than 2 per cent; by deficit spending the state can subsidize a low but stable rate of profit on all investment; there is apparently no limit to the amount of nonsense that people can be made to want to buy on the installment plan, mortgaging their future labor. And in fact we see, to our astonishment, that a large proportion, almost a majority, of the bourgeoisie are even now ready to settle for Plans that guarantee a low but stable profit. Or by collusion, a high and stable rate of profit. Shall we continue to call them bourgeois? They are *rentiers*.

The more dynamic wolf, on the other hand, is no longer a private enterpriser, but increasingly becomes a manager and administrator of the industrial machine as a whole: he is in the Government. He bares his teeth abroad.

ii. *Sociolatry*

With the conclusions so far reached, we can attempt a formal definition of the mass attitude that we call *Sociolatry* (after Comte).

Sociolatry is the concern felt by masses alienated from their deep natures for the smooth functioning of the industrial machine from which they believe they can get a higher standard of living and enjoy it in security. The revolutionary tension of the people is absorbed and sublimated by the interesting standard of living; but this standard is not physiological (which would be potentially revolutionary), nor is it principally economic, a standard of comfort and luxury (which would slow down the machine by breeding idleness, dillettantism, and eccentricity); it is a sociological standard energized by emulation and advertising, and cementing a sense of unanimity among the alienated. All men have—not the same human nature—but the same commodities. Thus, barring war, such an attitude of alienated concern could have a long duration. I say "barring war"—but we must ask below whether the war is not essentially related to the attitude.

On the part of the political elite: sociolatry is the agreement of the majority of the bourgeoisie to become *rentiers* of the industrial corporation in whose working they do not interfere; and the promotion of the more dynamic bourgeoisie to high-salaried, prestigious, and powerful places at the controls of the machine. Sociolatry is therefore the psychology of state capitalism and state socialism.

iii. *What Must Be the Revolutionery Program?*

Still barring from consideration the threat of war, we must now ask: what is a revolutionary program in the sociolatry? (By "revolutionary" I here refer to the heirs of Rousseau and the French Revolution: the conviction that man is born free and is in institutional chains; that fraternity is the deepest political force and the fountain of social invention; and that socialism implies the *absence* of state or other coercive power.)

For if indeed, with the steady expansion of technical productivity, the attitude of the masses has for a century moved toward sociolatry and the attitude of the bourgeoisie toward accepting a low but stable rate of profit, then the Marxian program is not only bankrupt but reactionary. The Marxian economic demands (for wages and conditions) cement the sociolatry; the Marxian political demands (for expropriation of the expropriators by seizing power) lead to state socialism.

It is with diffidence that I dissent from the social psychology of Karl Marx. When I was young, being possessed of an independent spirit I refused to embrace the social science of Marx, but proceeded, as an artist and a human being, to make my own judgments of the social behavior I saw about. And then I found, again and again, that the conclusions I slowly and imperfectly arrived at were already fully and demonstrably (and I may say, beautifully) expressed by Karl Marx. So I too was a Marxist! I decided with pleasure, for it is excellent to belong to a tradition and have wise friends. This was Marx as a social psychologist. But as regards political action, on the other hand, I did not see, it never seemed to me, that the slogans of the Marxians, nor even of Marx, lead toward fraternal socialism; rather they lead away from it. Bakunin was better. Kropotkin I agree with.

Now (*still* barring the war!) there is a great advantage for the revolutionist in the existence of sociolatry and of even a tyrannical welfare state. The standard of living and the present use of the machinery of production may rouse our disgust, but it is an ethical disgust; it is not the fierce need to act roused by general biological misery. We may therefore act in a more piecemeal, educational, and thoroughgoing way. The results of such action will also be lasting and worth while if we have grown into our freedom rather than driven each other into it. Our attack on the industrial system can be many sided and often indirect, to make it crash of its own weight rather than by frontal attack.

Nor is it the case that the absence of tension and despair makes it impossible to awaken revolutionary feeling. For we know that the society we want is universally present in the heart, though now generally submerged: it can be brought into existence piecemeal, power by power, everywhere: and as soon as it appears in act, the sociolatry becomes worthless, ridiculous, disgusting by comparison. There is no doubt that, once awakened, the natural powers of men are immeasurably stronger than these alien institutions (which are indeed only the pale sublimations of natural powers).

On the one hand, the kind of critique that my friends and I express: a selective attitude toward the technology, not without peasant features, is itself a product of our surplus technology; on the other hand, we touch precisely the vulnerable point of the system, its failure to win human allegiance.

Then, as opposed to the radical programs that already presuppose the great state and corporative structure, and the present social institutions in the perfected form of the Sociolatry, we must—in small groups—draw the line and try action more directly satisfactory to our deep nature. (a) It is essential that our program can, with courage and mutual encouragement and mutual aid, be put into effect by our own effort, to a degree at once and progressively more and more, without recourse to distant party or union decisions. (b) The groups must be small, because mutual aid is our common human nature mainly with respect to those with whom we deal face to face. (c) Our action must be aimed not, as utopians, at a future establishment; but (as millenarians, so to speak) at fraternal arrangements today, progressively incorporating more and more of the social functions into our free society.

(1) It is treasonable to free society not to work at a job that

realizes our human powers and transcends an unthinking and unchoosing subdivision of labor. It is a matter of guilt—this is a harsh saying—to exhaust our time of day in the usual work in office and factories, merely for wages. The aim of economy is not the efficient production of commodities, but co-operative jobs themselves worth doing, with the workers' full understanding of the machines and processes, releasing the industrial inventiveness that very many have. (Nor is it the case, *if we have regard to the whole output of social labor*, that modern technical efficiency requires, or is indeed compatible with, the huge present concentrations of machinery beyond the understanding and control of small groups of workers.*)

(2) We must reassess our standard of living and see what parts are really useful for subsistence and humane well-being, and which are slavery to the emulation, emotional security, and inferiority roused by exploitative institutions and coercive advertising. The question is not one of the quantity of goods (the fact that we swamp ourselves with household furnishings is likely due to psychic causes too deep for us willfully to alter), but that the goods that make up the "standard of living" are stamped with alien values.

(3) We must allow, and encourage, the sexual satisfaction of the young, both adolescents and small children, in order to free them from anxious submissiveness to authority. It is probably impossible to prevent our own neurotic prejudices from influencing children, but we can at least make opportunity for the sexual gratification of adolescents. This is essential in order to prevent the patterns of coercion and authority from re-emerging no matter what the political change has been.

(4) In small groups we must exercise direct initiative in community problems of personal concern to ourselves (housing, community plan, schooling, etc.). The constructive decisions of intimate concern to us cannot be delegated to representative government and bureaucracy. Further, even if the Government really represented the interests of the constituents, it is still the case that political initiative is itself the noble and integrating act of every

* This point is argued at length in *Communitas* by Percival and Paul Goodman, Vintage, 1960.

man. In government, as in economic production, what is superficially efficient is not efficient in the long run.

(5) Living in the midst of an alienated way of life, we must mutually analyze and purge our souls until we no longer regard as guilty or conspiratorial such illegal acts as spring from common human nature. (Group psycotherapy is identical with contactful neighbor-love, that pays attention and comes across.) With regard to committing such "crimes" we must exercise prudence not of inhibitions but such prudence as a sane man exercises in a madhouse. On the other hand, we must see that many acts commonly regarded as legal and even meritorious are treason against our natural society, *if they involve us in situations where we cease to have personal responsibility and concern for the consequences.*

(6) We must progressively abstain from whatever is connected with the war.

I am sensible that this program seems to demand very great initiative, courage, effort, and social invention; yet if once, looking about at our situation whatever it is, we *draw a line* (wherever we draw it!), can we not at once proceed? Those of us who have already been living in a more reasonable way do not find these minimal points too difficult; can those who have all their lives taken on the habits (if not the ideas) of the alienated society, expect not to make drastic changes? If we are to have peace, it is necessary to *wage* the peace. Otherwise, when their war comes, we also must hold ourselves responsible for it.

iv. *The War*

The emergency that faces sociolatry and state socialism is War, and we know that this catastrophe of theirs must overwhelm us all. Is it a necessity of their system? Must one not assume, and can one not observe, that beneath their acceptance and mechanical, unspontaneous pleasure in the current social satisfactions, there is a deep hatred for these satisfactions that makes men willing to rush off to armies and to toy with the idea of loosing explosive bombs?

(To put this another way: In a famous passage Freud pathetically justifies competitive capitalism as a means of releasing aggression without physical destruction. Now if, under improved economic arrangements of full employment and noncompetitive profits, this means of release is thwarted, how will the general aggression find an outlet—if the aggression itself is not moderated by small-scale fraternal competition, mutual aid, and instinctual gratification?)

We have defined a mass alienated from deep natural concerns, but occupying the conscious and preconscious with every manner of excitement, news, popular culture, sport, emulation, expenditure, and mechanical manipulation. Now let us draw from the individual psychology what seems to be an analogy, but is more than an analogy.

When an ego system is set up against the id drives, rather than as the interpreter, guide, purveyor, and agent of those drives, then this ego is basically weak and "tends to destroy itself." Further, the more elaborate the distractions sought by the ego, the tighter is the defense and rationalization against the instincts, the greater the tension, the more suggestive and hypnotic the daily unawareness, and the more inevitable the self-destruction. During the last years of his life, largely in order to explain the phenomena of war, Freud introduced into his theory the primordial death wish. But whether or not such a drive is really primitive (in general a hunch of Freud is better than the clinical evidence of a lesser man)—nevertheless, to explain the tendency to self-destruction that we are here considering, no such primitive drive is required. On the contrary, the rebellion of the instincts against the superficial distractions of the ego is a healthy reaction: it is a healthy kind of violence calculated not to destroy the organism but to liberate it from inanity. By the ego, however, this desire to "burst" (Wilhelm Reich) might be interpreted as the desire for suicide—and if the ego can indeed control the movements of the body and the imagination, that is in fact the end of the organism.

Let us return to the real social context (for all individual psychology is an abstraction): we see on all sides an ill-concealed—concealed only to those who are expressing it—hatred for the social satisfactions. The most refined champions of our civilized arena, namely the technicians and practical scientists, seem almost the most inspired to feverish co-operative activity if once it has in it the promise of violence. Further, the people as a whole can the more cheerfully rush to the destruction of what they have and what they are, because, inspired to it *en masse* and suggesting it to one another, they release one another from the guilty restraint that each would feel by himself.

The behavior of the Americans during the last interbellum was terribly significant. On the one hand, people were almost unanimously opposed to the coming war; there was even a certain amount of successful pacifist agitation (such as the barring of military training from many colleges). On the other hand, one economic and political action after another was committed that led directly to a worldwide war; and these acts were acquiesced in by the people despite the clear, demonstrative, and thousand-times-reiterated warnings from many quarters that the acts were heading toward a general war. It is absurd to claim that such warnings did not get a hearing, for the point is: why did they not? To me it seems that the public behavior was exactly that of a person in the face of a danger that he consciously wants to flee, but who is paralyzed because unconsciously he wants to embrace it: thus he waits and will not think of it.

But alas! this social violence that wants, not to destroy mankind, but only to get back to natural institutions, cannot be healthy, because it will in fact destroy us.

We others had better wage our peace and bring them quickly into our camp.

October, 1945.

6

Unanimity

In the mixed society of coercion and nature, positive political action is always dialectically good and evil. But nature underlies and coercion is imposed. Then we must act so as to avoid the isolation of a particular issue and the freezing of the coercive foreground, but always to submit the issue to the dynamism of the common natural powers that nobody disputes. The defining property of free political action is potential unanimity, drawing on common nature and undercutting the conflict of interests. Our political action is the emergence of unanimity from natural conflict. Many conflicts are wholly *theirs* and may profitably be disregarded. In others, such as the class struggle, where there is a direct attack on obvious goods such as sustenance or time of life, the issue is clearly enough drawn and we lend all force to freedom, justice, and nature. But where there is a natural conflict, between natural forces, the free man must not subscribe to a compromise but must invent a program, for natural conflict is solved only by invention, that introduces something new into the issue. If he cannot invent, it is likely that the conflict is internal in himself and inhibits his

invention; then he must withdraw to the sure ground previous to
the conflict where in fact he can invent.

i. *Dialectics of Positive Action*

It is unprofitable to strive, in coercive conditions, for a relative
advantage in a situation that, even if the victory is won, is coercive. Thus, to demand a just trial when the law to be executed is
unjust; or to exercise civil rights within the framework of the
State. To demand higher pay when the standard of living that
can be bought for money is unsatisfactory. To cry for military
democracy when the war is unnatural violence. This is wasting
one's strength and obscuring the true issues; it results in being
frozen and trapped.

On the other hand, since the strength and the continuance of
any society must depend on the naturalness of its conventions,
it is profitable to defend the natural conventions even with scrupulosity—though scrupulosity is most often avoided by the wise.
Thus, we appeal in the court as our court and enjoy the civil
powers that were liberated by our own great men; we bargain
because the marketplace has free choices; we demand a voice not
for the soldier but the man. (Yes! and the next step is for the man
to say "I quit.") This is essential to show that we are not alienated
from society—if not this society, what society do we have?—but
on the contrary, Society is alienated from itself.

The ordinary man is baffled by social dilemmas; the free man
must make social inventions that liberate strength. Nothing is more
disheartening than to see an honest party or press, unwilling to
lend itself to bad alternatives, that does not also continually produce a stream of good natural solutions. If a man cannot in fact
invent a way out, what right has such a man to be libertarian on
the issue at all? His negative criticism insults and disheartens the
rest. Further, it is not sufficient to proffer as a solution a state of
society and of institutions which is precisely not attainable by a
man's present powers of action; he must invent an action which
can be performed today. But indeed, *those who draw on natural*

powers find it easy to be inventive—on natural issues; a man who finds himself usually constrained merely to veto all the presented alternatives is almost surely coerced by unconscious resistance to some possible solution.

In natural ethics there is no such principle as the choice of the lesser of two evils. Such a principle is self-contradictory, for any free action or abstention must draw on natural power and cannot depend on a negation. When a social issue has come to the pass of a choice between evils (as, conscripting an army to resist a tyrant), then we know that the citizens have long neglected their welfare; the free actions that we can then invent are all attended with great suffering. They must involve withdrawing utterly from the area of guilt, a painful sacrifice—and more and more painful till all the consequences work themselves out. The lesser evil is a sign that an interest has been allowed to develop in isolation until it now threatens even our lives. *It is the isolation of the issue from its causes that restricts the choice to the lesser evil.* Those who break the spell and again draw on all their forces will find other choices.

Thus, to resist the greater evil it is usual for well-intentioned men not to embrace the lesser evil but to form a "united front" with it; in the feeblest case, such a united front is called "critical support"; in the strongest case it is based on a program of "minimum demands," presumably relevant to the causes of the crisis. Now, in principle a united front is nothing but mutual aid itself; but in practice it is often the inhibition of precisely the natural forces whose exercise would overcome the evil lesser and greater both. The formula of critical support usually comes to be simple acceptance. Therefore Gandhi said that by nature he was co-operative but he could not acquiesce to conditions that made it impossible to co-operate.

The formula of the "minimum program" is in principle the same as Drawing the Line: relax coercion at this point and we will co-operate, the presumption being that then the issue is no longer isolated and our action is not necessarily evil. But in practice this often comes to freezing the situation into a new coercive compromise and inhibiting the dynamism of the next step (but drawing the line is inseparable from the dynamism of the next step). The very granting of the minimum demands proves to be the form of the new coercion—otherwise it would not have been granted; as, social legislation prepares the corporate state. But social invention is impossible when the situation is frozen. Thus, with the aim of doing justice to the untouchables, Gandhi fasted against what seemed to be the reasonable minimum program of granting them a large number of sure constituencies in the Congress ("separate electorates"), because this would freeze their status as separate from the community.

In general, right action with regard to the lesser evil and the united front is part of what can be called "aggressive noncommitment" and "limited commitment":

Obviously a man cannot act rightly with regard to bad alternatives by simply not committing himself at all, for then he is in fact supporting whichever bad alternative happens to be the stronger. But the free man can often occupy an aggressive position outside either alternative, which undercuts the situation and draws on neglected forces; so that even after the issue has been decided between the alternatives, the issue is still alive: new forces have been marshaled that challenge the decision, except that now the challenger is not a bad alternative but an inventive solution. This is the right action when the presented alternatives are frozen fast in the coercive structure. On the other hand, when the situation is somewhat fluid or confused, the free man, "co-operative by nature," can make a limited commitment to a presented alternative, if (a) he can work to clarify the issue and (b) he can, if the issue crystallizes badly, withdraw still leaving the issue in doubt. He must retain considerable freedom of action; any free action, so long as it is exercised, will generate increasing power. The aggressively noncommittal man and the man who retains freedom of action when he commits himself to a limited extent will surely be effective and exert influence among those who are coerced, inhibited, and committed against their best nature.

But best of all is to act in situations where there is a natural unanimity and no need for either withdrawal or limitation, for such action inspires a man beyond his best judgment.

ii. *Unanimity*

Fraternal unanimity is the social resolution of a natural conflict better than the ability, desire, or judgment of the separate conflicting persons. For the most part unanimity is found not by relaxing but by sharpening the conflict, risking natural coercion, until the emergence of a new idea.

(I think it is preferable thus to define unanimity in terms of conflict and invention rather than in terms of the harmony of egos which, as I have argued against the revisionist Freudians, is narcissism and not a social relation at all.)

When the two parties to a conflict are in fact concerned for the common good, it is impossible that they should ever, unless for a temporary convenience, come to an electoral division and seek the majority. Each side will rather eagerly welcome rational opposition in order to perfect its own judgment. The conflict will generate a common solution, and the assent will be unanimous. This is of course a commonplace among bands of friends. When they are forced to a division and a vote, it is a sign that moral standards are at play which are outside the dynamism of the friendship. To be sure, in friendly groups many decisions become unanimous by default, when some of the friends are not sufficiently concerned to press their claim; but it is reasonable that those most concerned should win the decision.

Primitively the rule of the majority was, I suppose (without evidence), a tacit agreement not to fight the armed battle that the majority would win anyway. As such it is an obvious coercion that soon, moreover, becomes unconscious under the cover of an illusion of justice, fair play, etc. Some philosophical color of justice could be given the majority by the utilitarian calculus, that the satisfaction of many is better than the satisfaction of few, if only it were the case that the majority opinion generally turned out to their own satisfaction; but on the contrary, often the smaller the minority the more deeply considered its opinion. It is impossible that other things should ever be so equal that there is more wisdom in six heads than in five. Luckily most of the coercive conflicts that come to a vote are so nicely weighted with evils against each other that tossing a coin would also give a just decision. In practice, of course, the few are most concerned—either about the issue or just getting elected—and they have their way; the many default but regard themselves as uncoerced because they say Aye.

The general notion of a division and a vote would be ultimately justifiable only if there could in fact be irreconcilable natural forces or interests (then the agreed coercion would be better than the death struggle). But no such thing exists in psychology, and in social ethics it is a self-contradiction, for any free society springs from common humanity,* and any natural interest is not accidently but essentially related to this common basis. And what free man would rest easy if he thought that his friend had a value that he absolutely could not share, at least in sympathy?

"But," it is objected, "even if we agree that there cannot be any ultimately irreconcilable natural conflict, in practice there is always a temporary irreconcilable conflict: therefore we have de facto an irreconcilable conflict and consult the majority rather than the force of arms." Where such de facto conflict really exists, then certainly the conclusion follows. But in fact it rarely exists; almost always an inventive solution is at hand or close at hand. It is an illusion that in the kind of issues that arise in practical communal problems a *long* time, more than a few weeks or months, is required to hit on an inventive solution rather than a compromise or a bad powerful alternative (as if these were spiritual problems in which the soul must be tried before it comes to know); but it is precisely because the majority knows that it will have its way

---

* Yes; nevertheless, there are dilemmas in the human condition as such, because there are a number of "ultimate criteria" of right behavior which are incommensurable, and which in any given instance might cause an intellectually insoluble conflict. We say, "Let Justice be done though the heavens fall," even though justice makes no sense when the heavens have fallen and there is no society. A scientist is justified to explore further no matter what the consequences. Even a mountain-climber perishes in glory. An artist has an absolute mandate to finish his work even though his loved ones starve. And strong animal convictions, like love, friendship, loyalty, give a warrant for any excess. For any of these a man might blamelessly sacrifice his own life and jeopardize the rest of us; our humanity will applaud him. This is itself a wonderful property of common humanity.

that it inhibits invention and will not wait a single day. Was it the case, for instance, that in 1775 the Parliament did not have an inventive solution at hand?

Of unanimity itself, there is the natural and the coercive. Coercive unanimity is a political evil especially of modern times, though it has always had religious and military manifestations: it is the coercion of habits and unconscious forces so that the judgment of the ego comes as if spontaneously to assent. The classical instance is the hundred deep thinkers who explain in identical irate language that socalism would destroy their individualities. Natural unanimity relies also on unconscious ties—the creative power of fraternity goes beyond the abilities of individuals; they see their work come to be by surprise(and then they can explain it well enough). Bursts of uncontrolled social enthusiasm are also salutary, purgative and inspiring, and approximate the relaxation of the total orgasm; but—Lord!—not the settled and monotonous hypnosis, that both sustains and is sustained by many of our institutions of industry and entertainment—and often indeed without a personal hypnotist, so that coerced and coercer walk in one trance!

iii. *Positive Political Action*

We have been speaking of positive political action. Yet at least the word "politics" is anathema in anarchist writing. "Politics" is equated with coercion by the state apparatus and as the business of the group that is both the executive committee of the economic exploiters and practices exploitation on its own. This restriction of the term is unwise. For the fact is that throughout history, especially the best ages and many of the best men have spoken of themselves as political, and politics along with art and theory has been the noble activity of free men. Let us try to define politics as a free act, therefore belonging to free societies.

Anarchist writers often speak of "politics," the coercive functions of the state and the struggle for perquisites, as degenerating in free societies to mere "administrative functions." But in the first place, we can see today that it is precisely through administrative functions that the most poisonous features of state coercion come to express themselves. Secondly, it is false that such degeneration would occur or would be desirable. *Any measure of social initiation whatever, that is not routine and that faces initial opposition and must win its way to acceptance, is political.* Precisely a free man in a free society will often initiate new policies, enter into conflict with his fellows, and coerce them; but this is natural coercion.

It is best to define politics in the ancient way, as the constitutional relations among the functioning interests in a commonwealth. Then power springs from, and is limited by, function. The more modern notion of sovereignty, abstract power, is in principle illimitable, and in fact impedes function. It is imposed by pirates who are really outside the commonwealth; it is agreed to by neurotics who do not function of themselves and therefore have no counterforce.

A property of free political action is to be *positive*, in the legal sense of imposing a new convention. Here too the anarchists, true to their false intuition, condone only negative or abstaining political action, and they are justified by the centuries of unnatural coercive conventions. But it is not the case that out of day-to-day economic and domestic existence there arises any great thing without the imposition of a positive, yes even aggressive, idea. Consider the Zionist movement—to take an example from our coercive society: great cities have sprung up (some of them stupidly located), gardens have bloomed in deserts, and tribes of men have been set at rifle point; and all this is the effect of a mere idea in the mind of a journalist, working on prepared potentialities.

A free positive idea could be said naturally to coerce social forces into action—this is natural politics. A coercive positive idea will invariably inhibit or destroy natural forces—this is unnatural politics.

The alternative to natural politics is not no politics but coercive politics, for men will not cease to innovate positive social action. On the contrary, just the sentiment of routine and "administrative functions" invites bad innovations. Therefore we must speak of "waging the peace," just as we say "waging the war." The sense in which a free artist can speak of "arts of peace"—who knows what manner of peace one has with one's art!

Let me quote the great sentence of Michelet: "Initiation—education—government: these are three synonymous words."

To its initiator a positive idea seems at first coercive; then he recognizes it, perhaps only by acting it out, as the expression of his deeper powers, or sometimes of forces too deep to be properly called his own at all. If it is an idea that requires social co-operation, his fellows in turn will regard it as coercive. If then, as happens most often, the idea is erroneous—it is perhaps peculiar to his own nature or situation—their free judgment will safely resist him, especially since there are other positive ideas in the field. But if indeed he has a better reason, they must perforce again be naturally coerced; they are his pupils.

Civil liberty must mean the opportunity to initiate a policy, enterprise, or idea—this was how Milton or the early bourgeois meant it. It cannot mean merely freedom from restraint, as Mill seems to say, fighting a losing battle. Such liberty will not be preserved, except in form.

iv. *A Wrong Notion of Unanimity*

Just as there are terms unwisely rejected by our authors, so there are philosophers. (In principle it is unwise to reject philosophers, for what they say comes to pass anyway.) And the most rejected is Nietzsche. Nevertheless it is just the notion of Nietzsche that we are a bridge for who is better that can give salt to our concept of mutual aid. If freedom is the exercise of natural power we cannot avoid coming to speak of natural aristocracy; to do so would be precisely envy, fear, and, as Nietzsche would have said, resentment. Therefore we must say, "mutual aid *and* individual excellence"—and a moment's reflection will show that this is the same as saying "waging the peace."

Our fraternity that has more than its share of eccentrics! And what a pity if free societies failed to transmute strong eccentricity into exemplarity, but instead absorbed it. This would be the wrong kind of unanimity.

Strong eccentricity is the result in a coercive society of exercising any simple power too strong to be repressed. Since the system of coercion is organic and oppresses his power at every turn, hypocritically bringing it into "irreconcilable conflict" with other natural interests, the eccentric soon comes to deny that even plain goods are good. Thus we see that the gift of fearless speech, or strong animal lust, or common sense, all make eccentrics.

But in free society the strong power finds its relation to other forces; it tries to impose on them its positive idea; and it becomes exemplary of its own character. When the peace is waged, when there is individual excellence and mutual aid, the result is exemplarity: models of achievement.

v. *Another Wrong Notion of Unanimity*

A favorite saying of mutual aiders is "Happy is the people that has no history"—no wars, no dynasties, no need to rebel; and what is there in the round of sensible human existence, always springing from the same needs, to make a theme for history? Yet I should like to question this saying and distinguish coercive history from free history.

If we have regard only to the potentialities of human beings, it could be argued even that there has been no history, coercive or otherwise. In the thousands of years there is no sensory, scientific, ethical, or even technical capability that has evolved or been lost. It is always a common human nature.

(Indeed, the existence of a common unchanging human nature is an *a priori* principle of historical research—it is the true analogue, sought by Henry Adams, of the principle of the conservation of energy; it is by this regulative principle that the historian is confident that when he consults the documents they will prove explicable. If there had been changes in human nature, he would not recognize them anyway, except by lacunae in his understanding; but the justification of the principle is that in fact very few records turn up that defy some explanation or other in our terms, and further and more important, that the more faithful the historian is to the letter of the records, and the more he renounces "modern" preconceptions, the more recognizable the ancients become. By the same principle we also recognize our kinship to the lions and the bears.)

But now if we turn on the anarchist saying that the people is happy, etc., supposing we ask: what *is* this natural existence, what *are* these human powers, needs, and satisfactions that free society fosters? Then we see that we know them, in their fullness, only through history. History is the actuality of the human powers, and we infer the power from the act. It is Homer and Sophocles that demonstrate that we can be poets. From the peculiar character of an epoch we infer that certain powers, elsewhere actually expressed, were inhibited by the institutions. The university teaches where the creator spirit shone.

In the end, *it is only free positive action that makes history*, revealing the depths of our common powers. (So Marx, restricting himself to the consideration of man in class bondage, declared that history had not yet begun.) For in all the empires, systems of exploitation, and first, second, third world wars that make up coercive history, there is a deadly sameness: everywhere the inhibition of most of the forces of life and always the expression of the same trivial force. It is startling—and therefore their wars possess a melancholy interest—that even the Greeks, those inventors and sons of the morning, could not improvise anything better than this. But proofs, poems, heroic and saintly deeds, though there be many thousands of each, and thousands of each species of each, have all a difference and inventiveness.

Polity, too, is a free positive action, expediting, perhaps ennobling, the functioning of society. But it is dangerous; even without piracy, it soon hardens into abstract power. In the eighteenth-century American documents, of Jefferson and Madison, Adams and even Hamilton, it is remarkable how the authors speak as citizens, who embody the polity and are creating it as an existential act of their natures. But twenty years later, already in Jefferson's administration and disastrously by the time of Monroe and Jackson, the rhetoric is about "free" individuals patriotic to an abstract State that is not themselves.

June, 1945.

WINTER 1962

1

The devolution of democracy

Democratic power springs from an enlightened electorate. The neglect of this possibility in America, the failure to protect and advance it with new form and content during a century and a half of expanding area and population, of complicating economy and frequently revolutionized technology, and broadening relations with the rest of the world, has resulted in an electorate so demoralized that it is a question if it is possible to govern democratically at all. We tend to take lightly Jefferson's famous remark about the necessity for a revolution every twenty years, every new generation, but it is probably literally true, to renew democracy as he conceived it. (Jefferson was not, in fact, given to ill-considered slogans nor even dogmatism; but in stupider times his Enlightenment daring seems outlandish.) Meantime, during that century and a half, while the democratic power was being corrupted and was dwindling, other kinds of power and inertia have boldly filled up the vacuum, up to our present feudal system of monopolies, military and other bureaucracies, party machines, communications networks, and Established institutions.

The Kennedy Administration came in—one speaks as if it

were there a thousand years; will we get out of it alive?—after a marvelously established regime of business as usual. And it was going to "make America move." It would be a rule of things by active personalities instead of a bureaucratic staff; it would be a "disorderly" Administration, in the sense that ideas and people could leap-frog the chain of command and clash and have it out; it would be rich with ideas, as guaranteed by putting in or near power such notorious thinkers of new thoughts as academics from prestigious colleges. What the activity and thought were to be toward, what the purpose was, was not clear—there were no issues in the campaign, no effort to enlighten the electorate—but it was called the New Frontier. In this essay I want to show that this *image* of a government, of active persons with no idea, indeed fits the real situation better than its only rival did, and the voters were aesthetically wise to choose it—by a squeak.

After a year, including a Hundred Days and everything, and having learned that it is powerless and irrelevant except to "lead" in an intensified Cold War (which is itself, of course, powerless and irrelevant to any human good), the boyish élan is more sober. A philosopher close to the President now explains to me that the best to be hoped from government is to "mitigate the evils of modern life." This Niebuhrian political theory is not very wise, for if the aim is *merely* to mitigate, and not attack the structure and causes of the evils, one will not *even* mitigate, for the structure aggrandizes itself and produces new evils. It is as with civil liberties: if one merely protects them, without increasing the opportunities of freedom, one loses them. So I demur. I am then lectured to the effect that "if you had lived in the Administration of Jefferson, you would have been dissatisfied in the same way." That is, after a year in "power" under the present conditions, the Administration has begun to rewrite American history and prove that democratic power is a myth.

Since, by this philosophy, man is incurably stupid and his institutions evil, we must not get too hot to reform this or that present evil. And so they think. For instance, when three or four of us ask another Harvard professor to put a little zip into counteracting the nausea of the mass media—we propose to him a couple of excellent libertarian plans and are even ready to write the legislation and outline the campaign to arouse public opinion—we are treated to the popular wisdom that "people get what they want" and "what great art was ever produced by subsidy?" (Needless to say, however, when Cultural Freedom and the Encounter of Ideas are instruments of the CIA, means have been readily found to subsidize intellectual groups, even though nothing could be more treasonable to cultural freedom and the encounter of ideas.) But the problem, it seems to me, is an existential one; how does the professor, as an intellectual individual, keep down his nausea in front of the TV screen and not *have* to change? Presumably it is a government of men, and not an automatic machine, or what is the professor doing there?

Finally, on December 10, 1961, we have the answer in the Washington *Post:* Scholars in government "are good for ungarbling what thinkers on the outside have written . . . and tabulating the points" (Professor Schlesinger). I am breathless with the thought that Walt Rostow, etc., or even Arthur Schlesinger, imagine they can write more clearly than thinkers on the outside; but I am indignant that such good talents should be misused for writing précis; it's like the waste of skills in the Army.

After a year, the conception of a government of active personalities and disorderly clash has crystallized into the doctrine of the "Web of Tensions," the use of internal conflict to generate ideas. This Hegelian notion is psychologically correct. In the present ground-rules of the White House, however, it works out as follows: (1) There is a careful preselection of the combatants, so that no too obstreperous voice will disturb the proceedings, or laugh. (2) If anyone *in* the debate does disagree in a way awkward for the Cold War policy—and especially if his predictions prove correct—he is dropped. (3) At best in a megalopolis like the United States government, the Web of controversy is far removed from even its own staff workers, who nevertheless have to provide relevant materials and know what they are doing when they execute orders. To these workers the effect of the Web of Tensions is confusion, the feeling of purposelessness or divided purpose, of being out of contact and therefore absolutely frustrated when their earnest efforts are disregarded for reasons that cannot be explained to them. They then naturally withdraw into the usual bureaucratic apathy, now not even orderly. (4) Nor is this diffi-culty helped if the tense thinkers are by disposition in-turned, unfriendly, and unpragmatic. (5) Last but not least, the inventive outgoing moment of the Tension, the reason for it altogether, is horribly inhibited by the fact that the thinkers don't have any power anyway. As one critic has observed, the Web of Tensions simply means that they are getting more tense.

I don't want to be unfair, though it is hard not to be sarcastic. In the centralized power-complex that these people are committed to, and with the baroque conception of national sovereignty that they represent in a world that has come to have a different nature, it is probably impossible to govern. Both vested interests and the social-psychology of the people (and the influence of the vested interests in the social-psychology of the people) are fixed on the Cold War. Even the coalition that put Kennedy in office is too variegated to be maintained, and I shall try to show that he is re-forming that coalition to be a better Cold War "leader." The kind of revolutionary attitudes and do-or-die attempts at education that would make for government and tend again toward demo-cratic power are beyond the talents of these people; nor, of course, do they want them. They did not run, they were not elected, to thwart the "industrial-military complex," as the departing Presi-dent called it: to make peace and internationalize the world; to diversify and decentralize our economy; really to help backward peoples according to their needs and customs rather than for our own profits and war aims in alliance with their ruling cliques; to revive civil liberties and try to improve the quality of American life. They did not campaign for these purposes, but I am puzzled why, except for the politicians, they did campaign.

ii.

To get a better view of Washington after a year, let us turn from these Top philosophers to those who are not in the Web of Tensions, though not a thousand miles away. Here is a collection of comments:

"Lot of activism: action for the sake of action." "The way

they want to get something moving, you feel that they need to overcome something 'static' that is threatening to engulf them." "They don't know the difference between real power and the juvenile trappings of power." "As a matter of fact, there *is* a lot of loose power around, in Congress for instance, but he doesn't wield it. If some Congressmen had monkey-glands—"

"This Administration is peculiarly humorless, like phony actors. 'Posture' is the favorite word." "The preposterous syntax in the President's speeches: 'Ask not—' 'Let no one think, etc.,' especially when he occasionally mispronounces common words." "The worst was the speech to the Latin Americans, peppered with Spanish quotations but nobody taught him how to pronounce the words. It was embarrassing." "The Roman style is highly esteemed: tough, terse, we play for keeps." "I think they were badly stung by that remark last spring that they were great dribblers but never made a basket. I think that the need to produce at all costs was one reason for the Cuban goof." "Kennedy took full responsibility for it, like a Roman—and made full use of the scapegoat that he had poor Intelligence. But Bobby shut up the ones who apparently had more accurate information."

"They act on schematic preconceptions, with a crazy emphasis on Analysis and Facts. They have a justified contempt for the 'fuzzy liberals' who spout generalities that have nothing to do with the concrete situations, but they don't understand that you have to have an ideal, a pragmatic-end-in-view." "Naturally, being unpragmatic, they are continually projecting and finding scapegoats, rather than having real obstacles to overcome." "They are apprehensive of obstacles that don't even exist, for example, opposition in the Appropriations Committee on issues where there is no opposition. In my opinion, they do the same with the Russians. They never think of clearing up an ambiguity by going and asking; they always figure it out by Analysis and guessing. This isn't helped by an Intelligence that feeds them false facts." "They try to circumvent the preconceived obstacles by tricks. You get a memorandum an hour before the meeting, so there's no time to research it and back up your opposition. Perpetuation of errors."

"Kennedy is astoundingly sensitive to criticism in the press. Unlike Roosevelt, who got mad and told them off. But Kennedy

says, 'Now Jimmy Reston shouldn't have said a thing like that.' "
"He calls in *Life* to explain himself to *them!* So it becomes a sym-
biosis: since he takes them seriously, they are flattered and give
him a good press, and he gets sucked in." "Is he still worrying
about the close vote? Or maybe doubtful he should be there at
all? By the way, why should he?" "Kennedy believes that there
is a terrific force of reaction, that mustn't be confronted too fast,
and one mustn't go too far."

"Of course, in an enterprise this big there's bound to be confusion and bad communications. But it doesn't help when they
play it cool and by ear. Take the private-shelter story in *Life:* a
press officer gave it out and there was a howl afterwards." "In the
Eisenhower chain-of-command routine, there was at some level
a definite decision, also routine and usually lousy. But here one
doesn't know *what* has been decided, if anything." "If he had a
policy, why didn't he fire them all and put in his own people to
pursue his policy? How much obstruction can you put up with?
In three years Chile will be Communist even without Castro."
"The difference under Roosevelt was that the Secretary would
draw everybody together and inspire them with a pep talk; so
that in *spite* of the bureaucracy they pulled together and got going." "Well, in my agency the chief complaint is that there isn't
any contact with the bright young men who have access to the
White House. You ask, what do they talk about in the White
House? Oh, everything."

Finally, "There you are. All talk around here finally tends to
revolve around what He is like, and that's boring. Is it boring because we're sick of talking about personalities instead of issues, or
is it boring because Kennedy is boring? It comes to the same thing.
Kennedy seems to me to be simple." "Maybe the chief use of
this Administration, especially after the last, is that it shows that
livelier, better educated, and more likable people are even more
boring in this situation, unless they stand for something."

iii.

This is not a happy spectacle. Let me point out, however, that it pretty accurately describes the behavior of a crew of hipsters, as Mailer called them in 1960, not foreseeing the consequences. It is the cool and activist role-playing of vitality in a situation of impotence. (The impotence is caused partly by obstacles and partly by their characters.) Like the artist and live person he is, Mailer responded accurately to the type during the campaign; he missed its meaning because he is (transiently, I hope) a chump. More serious has been the error of the liberals who were "realistic" and who, instead of going about their business of dissenting and building a movement that they believed in, supported Kennedy on the theory that, once elected, he would drop the morals and techniques that got him the nomination. But to no reasonable person's surprise, the Administration proves, after the election, to have the same basic character as when the candidate was wresting the nomination and waging an uphill campaign. Being in office, however, is less favorable than campaigning for the display of jumpy vitality well heeled, morally uncommitted and intellectually shallow. Unfortunately, the end is not yet.

Of course I am judging by a high standard, but otherwise why bother? Why should these people seek office unless they had a useful idea and felt indispensable to execute it? Omit Kennedy and ask about the professors. They have given up citizenly independence and freedom of criticism in order to be servants of the public and friends of the cops. Presumably this is for the utility of power rather than the vanity of power. What? how? The answer is Analysis and Tabulation. In like manner, the scientists make bombs and missiles, but they do not make policy and they do not strike to enforce peace.

iv.

The impotence of the administration is due, I have said, to the past down-slope of our history and its present irrelevance to world history-making. These causes are intrinsically related, for if the United States were not the kind of society it has become, its Administration could work toward a world order. Our emergency is not in Berlin, etc., as the newspapers keep proclaiming but in the economic, social, and psychological need for the Cold War. If people attended to their real municipal and vocational affairs—if the TV and press were free—America might be less impotent.

With whatever hopes and purposes the Administration came in (and, as Oscar Gass has pointed out, these were already quite marginal and inoffensive to anybody), it has met the massiveness of the *status quo* and its established powers, venal, blimpish, police-ridden, prejudiced, and illiberal, officially existing in the Pentagon, the Treasury, the FBI, the Civil Service, the Scientific corporations, a large part of Congress. Eisenhower's Administration, in its personnel and motives and chain-of-command staff work, rather simply expressed these underlying existing forces and inertias; it therefore had—especially in the retrospect of having survived it—a certain solid impressiveness. The picture on the box was the same as the contents. With the best will in the world, the *status quo* is a rocky mass to move; but of course the son of Joseph Kennedy had no such foolish idea. His first official act was to continue the existing FBI and CIA, and that was already the end of working toward a new America or a new world. The Wall Street stalwarts—Dillon, McCone, Foster, etc.—were brought back as they would have been if Nixon had won. The Pentagon could become only more so. Inevitably the subordinates of the agencies would be unchanged, but in a large number of cases the same types were returned to make policy, or obstruct "policy." (Foreign Aid is a sad example.) Must we not assume that "tragic" bureaucratic mishaps and failures-to-communicate are importantly due to the persistence of forces that want no change?

So we are presented with the embarrassingly *un*impressive spectacle of impotence: an irrelevant activism, a "tough" "hard" "posture" (it is necessary to put every word in quotation marks), and an astounding timidity that results from trying to be different from their own class-strength and class-needs, although they have neither a new idea to give courage nor a revolutionary will to make a change. That, on the domestic scene, there *is* no such new idea nor will to useful change, you can observe by looking out the window or thumbing through *Life;* the scene is, as might be feared, the same, only a year more so. More big money, more unashamed tax dodgers, more cops, and more army. The war budget is at least 25 per cent more than Mr. Eisenhower's last; but otherwise the "public sector," that Ken Galbraith was vocal about, is not further nourished. Some in Washington say that the Education bill was beaten by a "tragic" combination of perplexities —Negro-white, parochial-public, poor states-rich states; others, however, say that Dillon couldn't afford it, that it was legislatively handled precisely in order to lose, and what evidence *is* there that Kennedy cares anything about Education? The *New York Times* has editorially described his interest as "tepid." That is, the program for a better quality of American life was fairly trivial to begin with (the liberals claimed that this moderation was necessary in order to win the election), but the will to achieve even this program has been lacking.

The field of action has been international affairs. It is estimated that three-quarters of the President's calendar is devoted to foreign and military matters, and certainly other matters are considered in this light, as fits the budget. The address to the Manufacturers strongly makes this point: when business is good, we look good in the world. Civil Rights for Negroes are never spoken of as social justice but always as enhancing our image in Africa and Asia. (I asked a young Ethiopian what *was* the image of America in Ethiopia; he said that the vast majority of his people never heard of America.) The pressing problems of Youth are recognized by the Administration either as delinquency to be handled by the Justice Department or in terms of the few thousand, FBI-screened, in the Peace Corps.

Yet here too, because of circumstances, action is impotent—except for the one grim potency of destroying everything. At present the administration of any sovereign State can make world-sense only by fitting into and furthering the inevitable development of the world community, and indeed by relaxing its own sovereignty. The interesting and long-range movement of the world has to do with increasing communications, exchange of people, the vanishing of colonialism and the rise of backward peoples from poverty, regional economic co-operation for mutual advantage. These secular movements occur, of course, according to their own laws, independent of Washington. A powerful national government can act in them only by contributing to them, perhaps leading. But an American administration is bedeviled in these things by business as usual and militarism, provincialism and jingoism. We cannot exchange goods with half the world; we cannot even talk to the Chinese. We cannot feed famine, though we have a surplus; we cannot give help to peoples except through our "friends," their rulers who rob them; and if a region is not a battleground, it is not considered useful to help at all. We put an ex-FBI man in charge of immigration. We cannot educate without propagandizing. We cannot engage in space exploration without competing, nor develop modern technology without polluting the atmosphere. We cannot strengthen the parliament of nations lest it evade our grip. And of course the behavior of all the other sovereignties—including new-fledged cannibals and feudal lordlings as well as tall generals and ideologists even crazier than our own—confounds the frustration.

The sphere of free action diminishes. Even Latin America is increasingly frustrating. The chief current idea seems to be the perfecting of the arrangements, begun by Truman and continued by Eisenhower, with the big new power associated with the Common Market. As McGeorge Bundy put it on December 6, 1961, "It would be better if Western Europe were one great power . . . with the economic strength, the military self-confidence, the political unity of a true great power"; and on the same day the President plugged for trade arrangements with Europa. (By the way, what will prevent French rights and German skill and money from becoming a third nuclear giant?) Bundy warns that our rapprochement with Europe might amount to a Rich Man's Club against the rest of the world—yes, so it might; but in terms reminiscent of the White Man's burden, Walt Rostow mentions the responsibility of the "North" for developing the "South." In my opinion this allied policy is better than Barry Goldwater's isolated fortress of America, but it will not exactly kindle the enthusiasm of the nations toward the peace and unity of the world.

But the chief outlet for frustrated action is, of course, armaments and threatening postures. Oscar Gass deliciously reports the expression "posture of sacrifice" as a threat. Most often, the style is that of a frustrated juvenile delinquent who fears he might be judged inactive and probably powerless. This is younger than hipster, but it must be remembered that in international affairs statesmen always regress to more adolescent attitudes, whether friendly or hostile. We play the game of Chicken. There is gloating that our "tough" "hard" "policy" has "won" in Berlin. Soldiers are mobilized and will perhaps be demobilized. We will have Bomb Shelters and defy them. *They* test their bombs, and *we* test our bombs. Walt Rostow is training guerrillas, since Castro did so well with them. (This is puzzling. Into what friendly countryside are the American guerrillas supposed to melt? Surely he means commandos?) The more hip age-level of the same frustration-syndrome is Game Theory applied to war. In Game Theory, the Web of Tensions is finally isolated completely from any contact with common reason, biological safety, or even any opponent except one's projections. All members of the Administration are experts in Game Theory.

A necessity for maintaining the Roman or cool posture is to have the situation always under control and not to be embarrassed by a goof or booboo. Unfortunately, this entails many contradictions. Since slant-eyed peasants are not really under one's control; since often one's best-considered efforts, as in Venezuela, work out opposite to what one planned; since from the beginning one is operating by a preconceived scheme, there are bound to be blunders and the threatening posture renders them more disastrous and more embarrassing. It is not possible to relent, atone, make amends, for these postures are "weak." On the other hand, to alibi, to be touchy to criticism, apprehensive of being misunderstood, fearful of future criticism, timid of commitment, forced to be consistent—these postures are also glaringly "weak." (One had the impression that Cuba, etc., was intimidating in this way, as if a gang suddenly realized they were on a tougher block than they had been brought up on.) There is then nothing for it but to strengthen reprisals and enlarge the arsenal. This is called the Cold War, and of course this has become the greatest frustration of all, since the final and only proof of power, to fight and win, entails suicide and losing. That is, the outlet for frustrated activity is a scene where activity is frustrated.

Gordon Christiansen, the chemist, argues that the newer tactics of the Cold War are *solely* for home consumption. Since the bomb shelters are scientifically fraudulent, they will not deceive the Russians; so their purpose, he says, must be a calculated deception of the Americans, to prepare for our making a first strike. This is too shocking to believe; and also, I think, it is too ill considered as a political policy for such astute politicians. Given the rising protest of so many respected scientists and students and even children, and many mothers, pushing the Civil Defense might result in riots on the streets. It is simpler to take it as the inevitable accumulation of frenzied expedients, as with the beast in Kafka's "Burrow." But of course this comes to the same end result as Christiansen fears. The breakdown of common sense and morals in the continuing Cold War makes it more and more indifferent who will be "guilty."

v.

As apparent from all the foregoing, the demography of the Administration consists of the *Status Quo*, the Coalition on which it was elected, and its own characteristic groups, viz.:

(1) Wall Street Republicans, continuing.

(2) The Pentagon, continuing, in which we must include the aristocrats of military science in Rand and Aerospace. These latter, since more mentally busy, are more bellicose than professional generals whose aims, on retirement, seem to be intensely economic and therefore they have an incentive to retire alive.

(3) Bureaucracy and Civil Service in the other agencies, also mostly continuing.

(4) FBI and CIA, continuing. These are, again, activist-violent in disposition. The FBI is more lower-class, the CIA more middle-class. But the aristocrats of the violent-minded are the new-come professors from the old OSS, trained in the prudence of Strategic Bombing. About half a dozen members of this Club have access.

(5) The fuzzy liberals, part of the coalition who don't really belong. But even Harriman would be called a liberal. (Reuther, of the UAW, is said to be a useful friend.)

(6) The professors. These are characteristic and fall into various types: e.g., Schlesinger, Wofford, or Galbraith more for thought and speeches; Rostow more for power postures; Bundy more for administering.

(7) A number of genuine intellectuals, interested in prudent and ideal action. These are mostly younger men—like the young instructors or assistant professors at universities, who suggest curriculum changes. This group is also characteristic of the Administration and gives it a livelier tone than its predecessor.

(8) The President's entourage for special assignments, with Irish names that roll on the tongue. We may here include Robert Kennedy. These are called, probably unfairly, the Irish Mafia.

(9) Besides, there is an unofficial night-life circle, generally upper-class and violent-minded. Important is Joseph Alsop who is said to leak hard-to-get data in order to push his activist policies and interests, e.g., the National Estimate of missiles. Alsop's tack is as follows: two years ago he said there was a missile gap, so we had to build fast; now he says that the gap was exaggerated, we are way ahead, so we can take risks. This gets you coming and going.

As might be expected, the glossary and style has strains of (1) Madison Avenue. E.g., "hard" and "soft" are applied to research, "hard" research contains numerals. "Shop," as "over in Charley Hitch's shop." "Sanitize" is very good: it means to doctor a report, as to Congress, to take out the virulence. (2) Rand Corporation: "escalate," "hardware," "parameters"—"what are the parameters of the problem?" A horror is "wargasm," meaning all-out retaliation, which I recommend to Mailer for his hipster theory. (3) Armed services: "tough" and other terms of panic about masculinity. (4) Lionel-Trilling-literary, especially "posture."

A curiosity that deserves special mention, however, is "exer-

cise," as "A crude propaganda exercise," referring to a Soviet
complaint about a Nazi in NATO. (British? I read in R. H. S.
Crossman, "The aim of the exercise is clear," referring to a book
he is reviewing.) The denotation is that the activity is only practice, it is not the real thing, it is not for keeps. Addressed to an
inferior in a bureaucracy it can be crushingly one-up, for it means
that there are grownups who do real things. But when used generally, as it is, it connotes that oneself is not *yet* altogether for real,
one is waiting to graduate and get to work. (This is strictly the
Cold War situation.) The next meaning—reinforced by the academic metaphor itself—is that *all* activity is merely academic,
detached from any serious possibility of life. Since it is necessary
to put up an appearance of being alive, one then adopts a posture
or stance. *But such persons could commit suicide.*

Finally, I must call attention to words like "discipline" "sacrifice" "responsibility" and "challenge," which in Kennedy's mouth
have a special stoical-Catholic tinkle. ("In this grave period, labor
must discipline itself—" "The press must discipline itself and assume responsibility—") This is not the Catholicism that was
touchy during the campaign, the prospect of Pope John in the
White House (oh, to have had that fat man instead of Kennedy
or Nixon!). It is the more moral Catholicism of the little boy who
disciplines himself from masturbating and checks off his victorious
days on the calendar. Masturbating proves you are weak and
makes you weak. In this context, "challenge" is the kind of strenu-
ous excitement possible to persons who, having given up their
internal spontaneity, rally to an external demand; and then (as
Murray Kempton judges) Kennedy is animated, genuine, physically courageous, and even unself-consciously humorous.

(To my ear, in the rhetoric of Kennedy's big set speeches, there
is an incompatibility between the two strains of the stoical-Catholic and the figure-of-history. The sense of duty does not seem to
be himself, but his submissive—and evasive—obedience to some
grownups; one is not convinced of his moral courage. The call-to-
glory is warmer and more personal, but it is juvenile. How can a
figure-of-history be spiritually inhibited? He cannot grow his
myth but must finally manufacture it. With the best efforts of

Madison Avenue and the History Department, such prose will
not turn to poetry.)

vi.

This brings me to the main theme of these reflections, the possible future of this character of Administration in our present democracy, the formation of what I shall call a New Consensus. We
have now had the Cold War for fifteen years and it is about time
that it became politically domesticated, with its own ethos and
personnel. In the present Administration we have a remarkable
and *organic* amalgam of the heirs and co-workers of America
First and McCarthy and the heirs of Democratic Liberalism. This
has an historical meaning. I cannot agree with otherwise excellent
observers that we can write off the New Frontier as simply another sell for business as usual, for history does not simply repeat.
Let me revert to my opening sentence, the failure of democracy
by neglecting to improve the electorate. We then have, in scheme,
the following devolution:

(1) For Jefferson, the chief use of democracy was *to* improve
the electorate and so itself; people learn by deciding, including
making mistakes. He championed decentralization, for people can
reasonably decide only what they know about intimately. Madison hit on federalism as a revolutionary device for experimenta-
tion, for if the small group made a mistake, it did little harm to the
whole; if it found something useful, it could be adopted by others
and benefit the whole. One is struck by the pragmatism of such
political thought, transforming the town meeting into an experi-
mental, self-improving unit with provision for expanding society.
Any basic function could be the principle for the small political
unit; e.g., to provide primary education, Jefferson suggested the
militia company or hundred. Applied to industry, the unit is the
soviet. The political units select their federal delegates; this is
democratic centralism from below.

(2) With the Jacksonian revolution, as de Tocqueville was quick
to see, the democratic idea was already abandoned, for the power

now resided in the majority of people *as they were*, with their passions and prejudices uneducated by the responsible give-and-take in a face-to-face meeting that had to make practical decisions and use tax money. Instead, the people would merely vote on issues and party programs. This was an invitation for demagogues and party leaders to get power, and for lobbying interests, that could deliver votes and cash, to influence the politicians for their own power.

(3) Through the nineteenth century, these nonpublic and non-governmental powers, bankers and industrialists, vastly increased their influence. Attempts to control them, e.g., by silver legislation and trust-busting, themselves centralized and increased the governmental power. But what was tragic was that grass-roots politics, like the agrarian and labor movements, also followed the centralized bureaucratic style. And of course the stresses and dislocations of war speeded up these processes. It is said that one reason that Woodrow Wilson hesitated to declare war was that he knew that the industries vastly expanded and empowered by war could never be displaced from power after the war.

(4) The imminent breakdown of the system in 1929 brought back a surge of popular participation in some respects not unlike the age of Jackson. But this was soon reintegrated into the bureaucratic central government by the paternalism of Roosevelt and his Agencies. Economic controls, social insurance, and other welfare began to break down altogether the formal division between government and the monopolies and other great powers of society. All this was regularized after the Second World War; by the 1950s there existed one massive Organized System, inert or expanding by its own law, immovable by any political public power, and administered, rather than governed, by the administration of Eisenhower.

(5) The election of 1960 was remarkable in that now there was not even the semblance of issues or programs for the voters to decide between. The election was importantly decided by the contrast of personalities on a TV screen. It was the end of the Jacksonian idea, since with mass communications and national commodities, people's passions and prejudices were themselves nationalized. There had ceased to be a democracy even in form.

The Administration would be, however, the necessary *symbol* of government. (For a rough analogy, consider the Roman "Republic" and its senators and consuls during the early Empire.) Now what are the characteristics of such a symbolic government, and what might be its future development?

vii.

Eisenhower was unsatisfactory in many ways. With all his solid virtues and genuine Rotarian togetherness and Everyman's ignorance, he was often ludicrous as a Chief of State. Newsmen had to edit him, satire had to be suppressed, lest the image of government break down altogether. Culturally, he was out of place as the head of a Great Power. But most important, his regime was universally regarded as dangerously boring. For two reasons: first, the public will to politics, whether or not it was possible to exert power, had absolutely no object on which to exercise itself. Discussions of domestic "policy" fell to an all-time low; and instead, there sprang up a vast literature of criticism of the System *en bloc,* of the Cars, the Organization, the Suburbs, etc., etc. Most of this was a one-upping cynical product of the system itself, yet it did express dissent and was disillusioning to the young. The later years of Eisenhower were marked by a resurgence of Youth, acting now in parapolitical movements, Birchite or Beatnik or Pacifist. But secondly, and most important, the adequate administrative inactivism of Eisenhower was symbolically quite inadequate for the affluent rigors of the Cold War. The old-fashioned diplomacy of J. F. Dulles, as brinkmanly as it was, still did not provide sufficient popular identification for so immense and continuing a deadlock. People began to join SANE.

It is essential to consider the social psychology of the Cold War. We must ask what are the moods and paralysis of people that demand such a sustained, pointless, menacing, and potentially catastrophic enterprise. I have gone into this subject frequently elsewhere—the exacerbation, in modern conditions, of masochistic violence, Enemy-projection, and paralysis—but let me here especially mention the public mood of powerlessness, powerlessness on the job, in the bureaucracy, before the TV screen, in politics, with the police; the sense that "nothing can be done." This powerlessness projects itself in the fantasy of the Big News on the Front Page, the terrific Drama of We and They mutually frowning for absolute stakes. But for this fantasy to thrive, there must be adequate Actors. Nixon plugged as hard as he could his *ad hominem* clash with Khrushchev, and indeed thereby almost won the election.

In all these respects Kennedy's Administration is a find. Kennedy can take care of himself in public and with his peers. His musicale has been praised by Paul Henry Lang who was so brutal to Ike. He is his own Secretary of State. His jaw is commensurate with General MacArthur's.* (Russian generals scowl; ours tend to jut the jaw.) He is vigorous and has physical courage. His lack of moral courage is no defect because, with Franco, Chiang Kaishek, and tommygun-defended bomb shelters, we are far beyond principle anyway; and on the contrary, a slippery idealism, in the style of Luce, makes a good hipster. We have seen that the Administration of active personalities *is* good; unlike with Eisenhower, the Game Theorists now seem at home. Yet the President himself is also a serious man, *sage* in the French sense, commensurate with the need for caution in the Emergency. He does his homework and learns the Facts. He is intelligent—not in the sense that we speak of our friends as intelligent, but in that he can read rapidly through a reasoned memorandum and catch the drift. Though he is high-toned himself, he has a nice family; his brother and sister-in-law have formed a study group in Fairfax county across the Potomac, and Professors Walt and Arthur are going to give weekly lectures.

Most important of all, finally; with the Kennedy Administration there emerges for the first time the possibility of a National Unity to "wage" the Cold War. There is no other figure whose background encompasses McCarthy (and so guarantees that he is not soft on Communism) and the Liberal Democrats (and so guaran-

---

* In the East Wing of the White House hangs a picture of the Great Stone Face. Considering the theme of Hawthorne's tale, this is really carrying the profiles of history to the point of juvenile *hybris*. Like asking Frost to alter his poem at the Inaugural.

tees that there will be no wage cuts during the war economy). For the remainder of this essay, let us trace the lineaments of the New Consensus as a further devolution of American democracy.

viii.

A new Center is necessary. We saw that it is in the nature of the Cold War, where there is aggressive activism without pragmatic power, that there must be blunders, embarrassing at home and abroad, and even economically injurious and so leading to panic among American businessmen who are notoriously unable to take the long view. Such things jolt public identification. Also, the present Administration came in not only with a tenuous majority but also by a coalition—e.g., of urban Negro preachers and southern politicians, of leftists and financiers—quite impossible to maintain. Within three months of being in office, Kennedy had lost the more earnest liberals who had supported him anyway only because of their congenital obsession not to leave a blank space on a ballot. He has lost the professors, scientists, etc., who protest the nuclear insanity. Youth has held on a little longer—with the Peace Corps and all—but is pulling away fast in all directions. (A gentleman high in the Administration has said that "Youth is not a class"; he is in error.) On the other hand, stalwart party liberals like Governor Lehman and Mrs. Roosevelt—and apparently even Bowles and Stevenson—*never* quit when there is the appearance of "influence" (they supported Wagner, and Mrs. Roosevelt is now for bomb shelters if they are community bomb shelters!). So the Center can go this far left. On the other hand, from the beginning Kennedy visited Nixon and Eisenhower and as far as General MacArthur. The plan for the New Consensus, therefore, emerges as follows:

(1) To drop the trouble-making liberals as quietly as possible.

(2) To exclude and ridicule the Extreme Right. The official stamp on this policy was the remarkable statement of J. Edgar Hoover condemning the rabid as unwitting fomenters of Communism. He sounded like the anti-anti-Communists of 1953.

(3) By a modest social legislation and a modest advance in Civil

Rights, to hold the unions and organized Negro groups, while reassuring business and convincing the Southerners that, in our world position, a progress toward desegregation is inevitable. With the stepped-up production of military hardware, there ought to be no increase in unemployment, even a decrease. Given this much and the continued support of, for example, Senator Humphrey (the Senator is alleged to have said, "When I accepted the leadership, I gave up liberal principles"), the Administration can rely on the ADA milieu of the New York *Post*, without impeding further gains.

(4) The true grandeur and security of the New Consensus come from these further gains: it is beginning to captivate the mass of lower-brow readers of the New York *Daily News* and the educated suburbanites who read Luce magazines and egg on their sons to get good grades and make the prestige colleges. These are the solid centers of Cold War fervor and Cold War mentality. The strengthening of the FBI suits the righteousness of the stupider and the conformism of the brighter. For the *News* readers, there is an advantage in the friendly ambience of Catholic humanism-plus-discipline, quite oblivious of any notion of civil liberties or social change; for the college-bound, the professors are reassuring of tolerance, and their schools are among the most prestigious. The amalgam of Murrow and Luce in Information has been masterly. To the horror of John Birch, Inc., the TV attitude toward the Communists is often understanding and almost admiring—they are a powerful enemy, we shall have to confront them for "a generation and maybe two generations" (I quote from a TV documentary called "The Remarkable Comrades"). It is now only the young pacifists who are treated sharply as naïve, misguided, and dangerous idealists. Persons like myself and my friends are gently encouraged as "utopians."

ix.

What is the intellectual Idea of the New Consensus? Let us go back to the Professors, who are not now class-objectionable because, in principle, everybody who is not underprivileged goes to college. First, they are not eggheads. An egghead is one who, seduced by intellect and truth, might by chance say something inexpedient or something poetical that illumines the scene. Also, they are not brain-trusters, pragmatists who might come out with future-thinking like the TVA or the uncensored WPA. Rather, as we have seen, the Professors do Analysis and Tabulate Facts. As philosophers, they affirm a broad tolerance of ideas and an absolute pessimism about ideal or "utopian" action. Thus, via Dr. Niebuhr, the sage of the *New Leader*, we get the astoundingly un-Protestant rapprochement of Harvard and the neo-Jesuits!

Washington at present has a pleasantly free atmosphere of discussion. (Naturally I do not know the tone in the middle of the Web of Tensions.) Unlike the previous crew, the professors know from experience that propositions do not bite, and they do make the best conversation pieces. I myself have been urged, by one who has access, to continue my indispensable "role of dissent." That is, we are the Jester. What is puzzling, however, is that the Administration is continually plaintively asking for ideas; the President asked even the NAM to send him ideas. The implication is, partly, that the carping critics really have no alternatives to suggest. The important fact is that, since the Administration neither can nor is willing to make structural changes, these people would not recognize an idea if they saw it. The openness to ideas, the hunger for ideas, in fact works out as follows:

When a radical reform is proposed—e.g., a concrete plan to countervail the technologized FBI or the mass media—at once one hears the most subtle niceties of definition and an amazing purity about constitutionality, possible corruption and abuse, the right of the public to "choose," etc., etc.; and anyway, as the clincher, Congress will never appropriate money for such a purpose. (As a critic has observed, "The wisdom of a policy is measured by the opinion of Mr. Oren Harris of Arkansas.") But if it is a matter of lending a much greater sum to a railroad that every banker has rejected as a bad risk, then there is no difficulty, there is a much looser interpretation of the public interest, and the Administration is willing to push. In the welfare state, there is a nice discrimination between expenditures that subsidize large enterprises and those that are worthless or peanuts. If the Public Sector means roads for

General Motors or Urban Renewal for Webb and Knapp, it is attended to; if it means community experiments, work camps for youth, public defenders, or even primary education, it is nicely scrutinized. (But of course this double standard of scrutiny has long been familiar to us in the mysterious law of Economics whereby expenditures in ooo,ooo,ooo, for armament, are never questioned with regard to nine or ten figures; expenditures for highways, in oo,ooo,ooo are rarely questioned for eight or nine figures. But expenditures for useful domestic purposes, in ooo,ooo or even o,ooo, are most strictly scrutinized; and, as poor people know, expenditures in oo or even o.oo require a means test and a quiz on morals.)

"Wagner is a hopeless boob!" exclaimed the Professor. "Then why did you support him?" "It was the chance of getting the Democratic machine away from De Sapio." "But it's *my* city!" I cried, "and you killed a strong reform movement." . . . Yet De Sapio *did* deliver New York City in the nominating convention, after oddly backing Symington, although any honest poll would have given most of the city to Stevenson. There's loyalty! To learn this kind of practical wisdom, you do not need to go to Harvard; you can get it in a pool room.

Let me illustrate the Higher Science from Aerospace, a wholly government-supported corporation. Attacking Kefauver's anti-drug-monopoly bill, the spokesman of Aerospace explained that it would retard progress in space exploration, e.g., in developing medicines for victims of nuclear fallout. (*Washington Star*, Dec. 10, 1961.) Aren't these people shameless?

Since I am nervous about the self-discipline entailed in the New Consensus, I ask about Civil Liberties. I am told, "Bobby Kennedy is not *against* civil liberties, he does not have any notion of what civil liberties *are*." I did not have the chance to see Harris Wofford, the adviser on Civil Rights, since he was out of the country. (There is no adviser on Civil Liberties.) Wofford is an excellent and thoughtful man; he has even written for *Liberation* about civil disobedience. But he is a professor from Notre Dame and his view on civil disobedience is that we cannot take away a man's God-given right to rot in jail (he does not go on to Hobbes's dictum that the State breaks the social compact if it jails you, and it's your natural duty to escape). But to my mind the most alarm-ing clue of what the Administration promises on civil liberties was its bland, and entirely innocent, proposal to raise the news rates in order to make the Post Office pay for itself! (This had to be dropped by Congress.) Yet one might have expected it: these people, professors of law and government and history, apparently do not have any notion of what the democratic idea *is*.

x.

The New Consensus is an ignoble prospect. It would also be dangerous; for if such a national unity can fully form, we shall drift into a kind of fascism of the majority. If there were then a major reverse—supposing Brazil, Chile, Venezuela would follow Castro—the United States would be a police state.

Robert Engler speaks of the society of the continuing Cold War as a "garrison state." I don't think so; it doesn't look like that. Rather, just the tightening of existing suburban conformism, grade-seeking education, FBI protection, and mass media, with a little addition of "discipline," "responsibility," and "sacrifice." This would be literally the despotism of the majority that Mill feared, manipulated by a popular Administration to meet a chronic Emergency.

In my opinion, the present Administration is committed to the Cold War (despite some evidence, I cannot believe it plans a first-strike nuclear war). It has no other economic plan than a war economy, no foreign policy outside the CIA, and no domestic idea at all.

If the Cold War is to be relaxed and catastrophe prevented, we must do it by action outside of their politics, by every means and on every relevant issue.

January, 1962

2

Some remarks on war spirit

In a disturbing study of the paralyzing effects of war spirit and war preparations, "The Arms Race as an Aspect of Popular Culture," Professor Robert Engler of Columbia warns us of the dislocation of scientific and professional education; the dislocation of the normal pattern of economy and industry; the growing spirit of the garrison state: censorship, lying propaganda, the infiltration of the (retired) military into the industrial system; the crazy competitive goals in armaments and the space race; the astonishing distortion of community values in the private-shelter business. People accept the whittling away of civil liberties. There is distortion even in the play and dreams of children.

We must ask also the opposite question: Why are people susceptible? What *in* our society and culture makes such a development possible? What paralysis in the public allows these preparations to become so deadly? It is a useful question, because to the degree that we can answer it, we can try to withdraw energy from the conditions and feelings that lurk in the background of the present spirit.

The economic advantages of the Cold War (to some) must be

mentioned first. And we may use economic policy as an unerring index of the secret position of the government in Washington. The government can protest as loudly as it wishes to the people of the world that it wants disarmament with inspection, etc.; but so long as there are no *actual* economic plans and preparations being made to reconvert industries to peacetime uses and to take up the slack of employment that disarmament would involve, we cannot believe the government. There are no such plans and preparations, though there is a Disarmament Agency and though Professor Melman has offered them a philosophy in *The Peace Race*.

John Ullmann of Hofstra has shown that even apart from the budget, our political structure itself predisposes us to the war spirit; for it combines prejudice and regimentation, self-righteousness and violence. And every study of the present regime in Washington shows that it has become largely a machine for waging Cold War. Even vested economic interests must succumb, for the government can make or ruin a firm by manipulating the contracts for armaments.

Let me now, however, go on to recall some psychological factors in the American cultural background that make the Cold War "advantageous." Our modern times are affluent and disappointed, active and powerless, technical and purposeless. This clinch *is* the Cold War.

In America, the so-called high standard of living, urbanism, the sexual revolution only partly carried through, have notoriously resulted in excessive busyness with little reward in happiness, and in excessive stimulation with inadequate sexual or creative discharge. People are balked by the general inhibition of anger and physical aggression in our cities, offices, and streamlined industries and grievance committees. And since one cannot be angry, one cannot be affectionate.

At the same time, as part of the same urban-technological-economical-political complex, common people today are extraordinarily powerless. Few ever make, individually or in face-to-face associations, decisions about many of the most important matters. Labor decides about neither the product nor the process, the utility nor the distribution. Affairs are bureaucratized, with inevitable petty delays and tensions. There is an almost total absence of real rather than formal democracy. A local meeting, e.g., a Parent-Teachers meeting, has no power to decide but can only exert pressure, which is usually cleverly evaded. Voters decide not issues or policies but the choice between equivalent Front personalities. The corporations dominate the economy and small enterprises are discouraged. The pattern, especially of middle-class life, is scheduled often down to the minute, and spontaneity is penalized. Even consumption goods are bought for emulation rather than final satisfaction. Police surveillance increases conformity and timidity. With increasing wealth, there is increasing insecurity.

According to the theory of masochism of Wilhelm Reich, which has become fairly standard, the result of such excessive stimulation and inadequate discharge is a need to "explode," be pierced, beaten, etc., in order to release the feelings that have been pent up. Of course, it is people themselves who are imprisoning themselves; they could release themselves if it were not for the totality of their fearfulness and ineffectuality. That is to say, they cannot release themselves. Instead, they feel that release must come from outside agents or events. More healthily, this is felt as excitement in destruction and danger; in the lure of daring and dangerous sports; in the innocent joy in watching a house burn down and living through hurricanes and earthquakes (and discussing them endlessly.) And characteristically of poor mankind, once they have been given the cosmical permission of Necessity, people act with the community and heroism that is in them from the beginning. The case is darker, more painful and sadistic when, avidly but generally more privately, people read up the air disasters. Likewise, the nuclear phobia of many patients is a projection of their own self-destructive and destructive wishes, and it vanishes when so analyzed, that is, when the patient can reconnect the images of disaster to the actual things that he wants to explode, burn, poison, annihilate.

Similar are fantasies of destructive Enemies, who will do the job for us. And it does not help if two opposed Enemies cooperate in their projections, so that each one recognizes a threat in the other and arms accordingly and so provides more tangible proof of the threat. (This phenomenon of mirror-image projections has been somewhat studied by Professor Osgood.)

A less familiar factor, but to my mind a very important one, is the inhibited response to the insulting and nauseating tone of our commercialized popular culture and advertising. People experience a self-disgust and a wish to annihilate, vomit up, this way of life; but they hold their nausea down, they feel powerless to give up this culture—it is all there is—they cannot even shut off the TV.

On these grounds, we can speak of War Spirit as an epidemic wish to commit suicide *en masse*, as one community. To have the frustration over with! to get rid of all that junk at once! Thus, an important explanation of the paralysis of the public in safeguarding against, or simply dismissing, the obvious irrationality and danger of war policies, is that people are inwardly betrayed by a wish for the catastrophe that they rationally oppose.

So far negatively. But there is a positive side. Powerless and uninventive in decisive affairs of everyday life, people increasingly find excitement in the doings of the Great on far-off stages and in the Big News in the newspapers. This occurs everywhere as spectatoritis and TV-watching. An event might be happening outside the window, but people will watch it on the TV screen instead; for there, it is purified, magnified, and legitimized by the national medium. What is sponsored by a national network is Reality. And, of course, of this Big News the most important is the drama of the Warring Powers, that toys with, and continually threatens to satisfy, every man's orgastic-destructive urges. Brinkmanship and Playing Chicken and the Testing of bigger firecrackers—however stupid and immediately rejectable by common reason—are nevertheless taken as most serious maneuvers. The powerlessness of the small gets solace by identification with power Elites, and people eagerly say "We" and "They," meaning one bloc or the other.

The outpouring of dammed-up hostility is channeled antiseptically and guiltlessly through pugnacious diplomacy, interest in impersonal technology, and the excitement of war-games theory. Push-button and aerial war is especially like a dream. It is forbiddingly satisfactory in its effects, yet one is hardly responsible for it, one has hardly even touched a weapon. Games-theory has the mechanical innocence of a computer.

My guess is that in the contemporary conditions of technology and standard of living, the Americans suffer somewhat more from the above psychological pressures than the Russians, who are still starved for consumer's goods and hope naïvely to get important satisfaction from them. The Americans have more need for the Cold War than the Russians. They can afford it more and, for the same reason, need it more. Since the Russians can afford it less, they also need it less. (I am told, however, that in Russia the big arms-production has gone so far that they too have an industrial-military complex that now goes by itself.) On the other hand—again this is my guess—in dictatorships there is more underlying animal fear, fear because acquaintances have suddenly vanished, fear of speaking out; therefore their War Spirit might involve more desperate adventurousness, more need for little proving victories, because people feel more inwardly unsafe. Also—this is said to be true of the Chinese—when there is famine and utter misery of life, it is only extreme actions that can weld people together at all. (The remedy for this is rather simple, to feed them.)

By and large, the panicky craze of the Americans for private, family bomb shelters seems best explicable in these terms. Because of the threat of poisoning and fire, public policy has come into an obvious clash with elementary biological safety. Yet it is impossible to change the public policy, and get rid of the industrial-military complex, for the war is wished for, and the identification with the Powerful is necessary for each powerless individual's conceit. The private bomb shelter is the way out of the clinch: It allows the war to happen, yet it withdraws from reliance on the Public Policy which is evidently too dangerous to trust. It is a Do-It-Yourself. It even somewhat satisfies the biological instinct for safety—if one reads *Life* rather than scrupulous scientists. Naturally all the better if the Shelters can then be harmonized with business as usual and become an emulative luxury, a part of the high standard of living.

The entire argument of this essay is summed up in the official bulletin of the Office of Civil Defense, when it says, "Fallout is merely a physical fact of this nuclear age. It can be faced like any other fact." Here we have the full-blown hallucination: dropping the bombs is thought of as a physical fact rather than a social fact. And also this outrageous and moronic proposition is swallowed like everything else.

But as Margaret Mead has recently pointed out, this private flight of the Americans into their shelters has aroused shock and horror in the Europeans who are equally endangered. *They* cannot identify with the Powers; and many of them—British, Dutch, Russians—know what it is to be bombed and suffer in the war. (The Germans seem to be eager to assume the Bully role again themselves.) Naturally, Professor Mead's solution is international bomb shelters for the fertile and academically talented!

Historically, the theorists of militarism have profited by the above analysis. From the time of Frederick William, the gait and posture of the warrior has been designed, by competent teachers of gymnastics, to cut off full sexual feeling and tenderness: the pelvis retracted, the anus tightened, the belly hardened, the exhalation impeded by squaring the shoulders. Marriage and other civilian ties are discouraged (but not the economic and political connections of retired generals). A soldier or sailor on the town must not become emotionally involved with the woman he picks up. And the Marine, balked in his manliness and insulted in his independence by spirit-breaking discipline and the chain of command, lives by a conceit of toughness and power, with slavish griping to let off steam. All are in a state of muscular hyper-tonus, to snap unthinkingly to a command. The jaw is in a position of watchfulness. The public glorification of this mindless power is the complement of the public masochism; it is experienced as the terrible sublimity of war.

What then? How under modern conditions can we wage peace instead of war? We need a vast increase in the opportunities for initiative and making important decisions. This involves considerable decentralization of management, in industry, in government, in urban affairs like housing and schooling. (I do not think that this necessarily implies less efficiency, but that is another story.) It involves the use of our productivity to insure minimum subsistence, but otherwise the encouragement of individual enterprises. We must forthrightly carry through the sexual revolution, encourage the sexuality of children and adolescents, get rid of the sex laws and other moral laws. Many people might be offended by this policy, it might have disadvantages, but our present condition of stimulation and inadequate discharge is simply too dangerous in its irrational effects; we cannot continue it. We must revive individual worth and self-respect, by jobs of useful work that employ more of each person's capacities, and an education that makes the culture and technology comprehensible and appropriable, so that people may be at home with it and possibly inventive and creative in it. We need a genuine folk-culture to enliven community, and a lofty public culture to give us meaning, and loyalty to a greater self. And paradoxically, if there were less false politeness, conformity, and civil peace—more energetic confrontation, loud quarrels, and fist fights—there would be less ultimate and catastrophic explosiveness. These things comprise, in my opinion, the modern moral equivalent of war that William James was after. They are entirely practical; and if, as the Americans are, they are utopian—there it is.

An occasional fist fight, a better orgasm, friendly games, a job of useful work, initiating enterprises, deciding real issues in manageable meetings, and being moved by things that are beautiful, curious, or wonderful—these diminish the spirit of war because they attach people to life. They should not be postponed while we "buy time" with deterrence and negotiations. On the contrary, if people began to insist on more life, the Front Page would carry very different news.

Let me add a postscript. I read these remarks to a conference of learned men, experts in the social sciences, in engineering, and in politics, discussing the deadly danger of the Cold War and the need to get out of it. The great majority of them found what I said to be entirely irrelevant. They were, predictably, hilarious about the references to sexuality. We are faced with an unexampled situation, a matter of life and death, publicly apparent to all the people and to which people hardly respond. Yet these experts believe that the concrete facts of people's lives are not involved at all. Being superstitious as only modern scientists can be, they believe that something comes from nothing. Presumably, none of these facts of a life worth living are existent facts for them

—not when they are "thinking." They are "practical": they face the issues as presented. Presented by whom? why?

One scientist, from Washington, spoke up and said: "You say that the Americans have a neurotic feeling of powerlessness. You don't realize that those in power are equally frustrated."

3

For Tom

As if I have resigned myself to dying—I no longer strive against death, as I used, by making poems. Instead, week after week I go in airplanes to distant colleges and cities and make speeches and excite the students. My subjects are political, but I rarely teach; I am usually quarreling and fighting. I no longer have many thoughts of a bright world. All this polemic and fighting is noise. Sometimes, however, my eyes water at a sensible proposal for the future, whether by myself or somebody else, or the thought of a magnanimous deed.

Yet this harshness I feel cannot be what I give, for everywhere people thank me and love me and say my presence has made them lively. (If any fear or hate me, they do not come to me and tell me so.) The United States and Canada are dotted with friends to whom I am important, so many that I cannot remember them. Perhaps my mission is meaningful. But to me it passes like a dream; I was noisy there but it is as if I had not been there. Lately I have been too exhausted to invent new speeches and I repeat myself, sick of the sound of my voice.

They sometimes pay me well and therefore respect me as part of their Establishment. I am greedy for money but I have enough. Maybe I go because I am not doing anything else to justify me. Also, having been long neglected, now I can't say no, but like a jealous child I am afraid to leave the place empty for another. Yet when I am there, I have nothing to say but the truth as I see it. I have no ax to grind nor job to seek. These things give my words and behavior a random freedom that unsettles people.

What am I doing, as I go about quarreling and exhorting, out of touch with my creative soul? I am delivering my insensate body to a clash with the powers of the world. I behave without diffidence because they have invited me, I am not imposing. By both my words and actions—frankness, indignant outbursts *ad hominem*, compassionate attention, sexual advances—I seem to be defying them to take revenge on me, though I am a coward about blows and jail. Indeed, I have a way of picking my fight on the exact spot: I attack the TV screen on which I am appearing, or the Commissioner of Education who has just pompously introduced me on the platform. As yet I take them by surprise by my bad manners and they have not struck. When they do, I shall have no resources of my own, but stand with empty hanging hands. Will the many friends that I think I have made then come to my defense?

Why do they call on *me*, though they know beforehand that I'll make trouble? They seem to be longing for the Reformation.

Wherever I turn in my country, I see the Whore of Babylon. The venal, insulting, shoddily glamorous mockery of our humanity. Here is a brochure advertising shelters against atom bombs as "a new concept in convenience, combining the security and protection your family deserves with the comfort and pleasure of a new room for family living." It is nauseating. I am deeply ashamed for us. Men have no right to insult mankind so. I feel choked. I must protest. The holy spirit in me no longer has any other voice.

Last week I implored the young pastors of the Lutheran League to declare a day of mourning for mankind and these bombs. But they are hopelessly bound in their conventionality. I have more

hope of the young teachers and students in the universities to rally
to common reason and say, "We've had enough of this nonsense,
cut it out."

Three Sonnets

1959

Their theater! their businesses! their State!
it is the Whore of Babylon again
falser than Rome, and fewer are the men
not turned to swine. Her streets asphyxiate
honor, and literature is lying prostrate
in mud on Madison Avenue that "fen
of stagnant waters," while the denizen
hoodlums prowl with boot and chain and switchblade.

The witnesses are few. Convenient
allies, thank God, have vanished at midnight
and we are marked for oblivion who dissent.
So they believe, but an uncanny light
is shining on our faces at the faint
dawn bugle when the things fall of their weight.

October, 1961

My poisoned one, my world! we stubborn few
physicians work with worried brows and speak
in low voices; dying in the epidemic,
our quiet will is only what to do.
The time is Indian summer and the blue
heaven is cloudless, but the rains will reek
with poison and the coming spring be sick,
if fire has not blasted us in the snow.

The virtue of a physician is compassion.
We do deny that you are as you are
and work to make you otherwise. Creator
Spirit come, and join our consultation:

we do not have the leisure to despair,
we cannot cope without new inspiration.

April, 1962

My countrymen have now become too base,
I give them up, I cannot speak with men
not equal to me. I was an American,
now where to drag my days out and erase
this awful memory of the United States?
what can I work at? I hired out my pen
to make my country practical, but I can
no longer serve these people, they are worthless.
"Resign! Resign!" the word rings in my soul
—is it for me? or shall I make a sign
and picket the White House blindly in the rain,
or hold it up on Madison Avenue
till I can vomit, or walk to and fro
gloomily in front of the public school?

4

On the worldwide general strike for peace

The unique situation of the worldwide Cold War must involve a revision and extension of basic juristic and political ideas. The following are a few broad philosophical considerations that have led me to be a "sponsor" of (be answerable for), and to take part in, the recent "Worldwide General Strike for Peace." This apparently pompous name is quite unhistorical, yet it is not inappropriate to the new circumstances.

Let us assume first a contractual, rather than an organic, theory of fundamental law: In this ideal model of rational persons making free choices, people submit to the rules and restrictions of Society in order to protect their lives and liberties and to avoid disorder and unnecessary conflict. As a decentralist and community anarchist, I of course believe that these rules are too numerous and the sovereignty of Society is too strict; indeed, if we had fewer and less coercive laws, we should need them less, since the laws themselves create much of the disorder. Nevertheless, in any complicated community, the institutions and objective customs are the way by which people do understand and accommodate to one another and work together: they are the "social compact." The opposite condition, called the "state of nature"—mythically, for there is no people in such a condition—is one in which life would be, as Hobbes said, nasty, brutish, and short.

But if the institutions of society become themselves dangerous to life and liberty, then the social compact is dissolved, it has lost its justification. For example, according to Hobbes again, if a man is imprisoned (and so the social compact is dissolved), he has a moral duty to try to escape, as a natural animal. The same reasoning has been used to justify revolution, when institutions are intolerable. A kind of proof of intolerability is given when people in fact do not tolerate them and succeed in replacing them.

The emergency of the Cold War is, unfortunately, rapidly becoming a black-and-white case of dissolution of the social compact. The poisoning of the atmosphere by nuclear testing; the accelerating accumulation of armaments that, by intention or not, will surely explode; and the tantrum diplomacy that must hasten the debacle, threaten imminently to destroy life, not to speak of liberty. If we may judge by the morality of the tommy-gun-defended private fallout shelters of last year, our life is becoming worse than nasty and brutish, and will not even be short. We are thus driven to think of refusing to co-operate with institutions of society so irrational that they undermine the basis of any society whatever.

This society-destroying property of war is not new. Certainly World War I and II, with their attack on civilians and massive bombings, have brought us to our present lawlessness. War of this kind is not a political policy; it has no pros and cons for persuasion. But the Cold War, finally, confronts us with an absolute biological emergency. The only response to it is the rational-animal response of saying, No. We won't go along with it. Stop it.

The term "general strike" used to refer to an all-embracing power-conflict short of violence, in a showdown between classes or parties for political control. In the face of nuclear war, however, the showdown has become a chronic acute emergency. We are forced to act, though few, as if it were a showdown in the minds of many; for it is in fact a showdown for everybody. Also, there is not, primarily, a conflict for political control. Everybody is equally threatened; the powerful are made powerless by the clinch of the danger. So the general withdrawal of co-operation is not, essentially, a weapon against the dominant power in order to replace it, but an act of common reason and imagination against the whole political structure, to relax the danger, *even though no rival structure is clearly envisaged.* (Let me return to this later.)

We have been assuming a contractual theory of society. It is more realistic, however, to assume a more "organic" theory: that people exist in society by bonds of animality, fellowship, and obedience that are broader and "deeper" than rational choice. But all the more spectacularly, in the biological emergency of the Cold War, these bonds also are loosed, by revulsion, fear, and indeed a sense of the eerie. It is impossible, for instance, to hear a group of professors and scientists discussing war games-theory and mega-corpses, without feeling that they, although rational men, are moving in a paranoid system, toward which the only therapeutic stance is a kindly but firm negative. Their institutions have become altogether alienated from any natural community. The massive reaction to the testing a few years ago, which led to the great initial success of SANE, was certainly due to the revulsion against poisoning. But even more significant of the weakening of the social fabric is the spontaneous and highly *dis*organized formation of small protest groups everywhere, thousands of ordinary people finding courage in their friends and neighbors to perform acts of nonconformity.

The belief of people in their official leaders is unable, over many years, to bear the strain of their patent fraudulence. When 353 sessions of experts cannot decide on an inspection procedure and break up in flat failure, one must conclude that there is no will to succeed and agree. And besides these complicated negotiations, there are several simple ways to relax the Cold War. The ingenious scheme of Charles Osgood to relax distrust and tension; Stephen James's dumb-bunny proposal to revive the medieval exchange of hostages—such things have the virtue of calling the bluff; they would safely and cheaply bring peace; there is no necessity for armed "deterrence." But the governments do not will peace. Even worse in arousing disbelief, the evident scientific quackery of our government in its shelter pronouncements, manipulation of the "safe" fallout levels, disregard of the seismological facts relating to inspection, secrecy about experiments well known to the international scientific community, can have no other meaning than the wish to deceive our own people.

ii.

In the world community—of communications and travel, technology and industrialization, and the responsibility to help backward regions—the national sovereignties are a baroque hangover. There might be some shadow of a reason for the transient existence of the new sovereignties of Africa and Asia in their emergence from colonialism; but on the whole this imitative evolution is an absurdity. Our own President and his associates are in principle little different from Louis XIV, and the Russian regime still reminds one of Peter the Great, unchanged, in this respect, by the October Revolution. Naturally, in their senility the states exaggerate their worst archaic features, the cult of personality, the dead weight of bureaucratic routine, the tendency toward monopoly. The arts cannot lie; the newer official buildings of Washington, Moscow, or London give one a sense of crashing futility— worse than the positive ugliness of the Hohenzollerns and Hitler or the childish grandiosity of Victor Emmanuel and Mussolini. This idea can no longer renew itself.

The very futility of the States, however, commits them rigidly to the Cold War. Without it, it is doubtful if the great sovereignties could survive with anything like their present personnel, vested interests, motivations, and ideology. Their one function seems to be to continue a clinch and hinder the evolution of the world community. And, of course, domestic and economic policy are swallowed up by the Cold War. Twenty per cent of the gross national production is devoted more or less directly to armament, and we are drifting rapidly forward into a fascism-by-consent.

The case is not different in Russia, except that Russia can afford it less. American statesmen eagerly wait for the Russians to crack under the strain; they point out (truly) that a declaration of peace would be to Russia's advantage. The Russian leaders, on the other hand, seek out and foment troubles anywhere in the world, in order to fish in muddy waters.

Such a rigidifying, and already almost absolute, commitment to the Cold War cannot be altered by ordinary political means. In our country, petitions are ignored or lied to; the official parties, and the mass media, put forward rival candidates who are equally Cold Warriors, so voting is meaningless. Thus people must engage in actions like this strike. We are doing so. Sporadically— in neighborhood walks and trainloads of mothers; in the antiwar use of class time by a hundred young instructors and a protest signed by a thousand senior professors; in the refusal of shelter drills by children, the ingenious trouble-making of "nonviolent youth," and vigils by the conscience-stricken. These events become more frequent. The numbers involved become greater. There is a remarkable spontaneity. Organization is never more than ragged and usually it is *ad hoc*. A biological and moral reaction and good sense seem to be enough to arouse people, once it is suggested, and if they encourage one another in small groups.

Like the community itself, the nuclear danger is worldwide, and the protest is worldwide. There have been great popular protests in England, Scandinavia, and Africa, and Japan. About the Soviet bloc we do not know, but the government had to try to keep its recent testing secret from the Russian people. If there is testing from Christmas Island, we can expect protests from the Indians and South Americans. But of course the people of the United States have a peculiar mission to lead this movement; the bomb was our baby and we first made it mighty. Conversely, the almost uniquely American talk of shelters must rouse universal disgust.

iii.

The peace movement is at present astoundingly negative: "strike for peace" means merely "refuse the Cold War." The most popular slogan is Ban the Bomb, and there is a rising realization that Peace Must Come from the People. But the idea of positively waging peace—in acts of community-forming, new culture, political reconstruction, economic conversion—seems not yet to take hold of the popular feeling. Yet it is psychologically and sociologically evident that the war spirit is energized by profound frustrations and anxieties of moral and civil life; that the extraordinary apathy of the vast majority to their danger is a result of institutions that have fragmented community and made people feel powerless; and that the only economy possible, under the present control, is the Cold War economy. Really to relax the Cold War requires withdrawing energy from its causes. Hard thinkers in fact propose real satisfactions, more practical institutions, a productive use of technology, and so forth. Yet these ideas are not importantly part of the peace movement. Apparently it is first necessary, at least in America, for hundreds of thousands of people to break loose, by merely negative action, from the mesmerism of affluent powerlessness. The decision-makers in our society, whether in the economy or in politics, seem to be simply in the grip of greed, stupidity, and timidity; and everybody, including the decision-makers, is in the paralysis that comes from wishing for a liberating catastrophe. All, then, deny their personal impotence in fantasies and enjoy the cheap excitement of being actors in the dramatic battle of the Giants. This impotence *is* the Cold War.

To the extent that the refusers have escaped from this mesmerism and this fantasy, and returned to normal fear and sense, they have already done a lot of positive psychic and social work.

In the course of time, so much spontaneous action as we see occurring must also generate a political idea. But the attempt, e.g., by Leo Szilard, to create a political party for peace as such seems to be irrelevant, since the movement grows anyway. My guess is that a more positive political idea will begin to occur to people when the strike finally begins to reach the labor unions and to be a serious threat to important parts of the economy. For when it becomes clear that we will not continue to organize our purpose, work, and livelihood as at present, we shall think how we ought to organize them. Naturally, my own hope is that, having gotten a bellyful of centralized managerial capitalism and mass-media democracy, people will rally to decentralized economy and politics and communitarian ideals. But although the peace movement cuts across class lines, color lines, and national lines, and is non-conformist and raggedly organized, I do not as yet see that it presages any particular political shape.

iv.

Perhaps there is a spiritual travail still to be undergone before people can conceive a creative idea, just as, after a loss, it is necessary to go through mourning-labor before one can again think of living on.

It is twenty years since we—I speak as an American—prepared and then dropped the bombs on Hiroshima and Nagasaki. Quite apart from the question of the right or wrong strategy of those acts, the fact remains that now we and the rest of the world exist in anxiety and danger because of them. From the aspect of eternity, it is impossible not to see this arc of events as a tragic retribution. He that takes the sword will perish by the sword.

It is not to be expected that the plight in which we have plunged ourselves can be evaded by game-theory or negotiations. It requires deep mourning, thoughtfulness, and hard labor to undo. There will have to be important changes. What is to be mourned for and thought about and undone, is how we live and what it has brought us to. By and large we have not been happy, and we live in fear.

In these twenty years, we have not heard such mourning begun by Mr. Truman, Mr. Eisenhower, or so far by Mr. Kennedy. We have not heard it from the churches or universities. But evidently many of the people of the peace movement, especially the older ones, have been mournful and thoughtful, and all are engaged in the hard labor to undo.

5

The ineffectuality of some intelligent people

At their meeting in 1960, the American Association for the Advancement of Science proposed that it was the duty of scientists to inform the public of the dangers of the bomb-testing and "the 99 per cent probability of the bombs going off within ten years." I asked Margaret Mead—who had been one of the leading figures—if this meant that scientists working to produce these deadly products should quit their jobs. "Certainly not," she said; "it is their duty as scientists to inform the public." But what simple soul would then believe them? or, if one believed them, how to regard them except as monsters? The theory, apparently, was that the public, if informed, would exert pressure on the governments; but the scientists did not exert the pressure that *they* had. "Why don't the American and Russian scientists, who are so friendly," I asked, "strike, exert their power, put a stop to it?" "That would be conspiracy," said Professor Mead tartly. So it would.

I am again and again baffled how persons of intellect, of good intention, of strong conviction, reason in a way that must logically lead to an action, and yet do not act. This seems to me to be profoundly pathological, yet how to cure it? Such people are not hypocritical, so one cannot expose and shame them. I do not believe that they are merely timid and afraid of losing their jobs. They do not seem to suffer from the despair that nothing can be done, since they speak up and urge us to do this and that. But they themselves seem to have lost the spring of initiative, the ability of moving themselves, which Aristotle singled out as a chief property of living animals.

i. *Unitarians, etc.*

To explore this pathology of professors and scientists, let us first consider a (perhaps) simpler group of well-intentioned, intelligent, solid citizens, whose ineffectuality seems to be explicable on more familiar social grounds. This group we may loosely identify as Unitarians, Universalists, Humanists, members of the Ethical Culture Society, many Quakers. They are more than a hundred thousand, educated far above the average, richer than the average, with considerable moral courage and high ideals of life. Why do they throw so little weight? We can think of half a dozen reasons.

In the first place, they have a defect of their virtues: they are decent and observe the rules of the game, even when the rules are manipulated against them. Suppose, for instance, they have been vehemently opposed to the bomb shelters, following Mrs. Roosevelt, whom many of them respect as a leader. Nevertheless, when the government, by its characteristic arts of crash publicity and scientific quackery, manages to set moving a shelter program with popular acquiescence, soon our friends, again following Mrs. Roosevelt (and Margaret Mead), bow to the "democracy" and agree to the bomb shelters if they are *community*, rather than private, shelters. Contrast with this the behavior and success of high-school youngsters in the New York City schools. A couple of years ago, to protest the shelter drills, the students wore blue armbands, although that was forbidden; and in one school a few were suspended. By the next semester, the youngsters refused to participate in the drills altogether, and the principal of one school now *asked* them to wear blue arm-bands to register their protest. But the students persisted in boycotting the drills and again a few were suspended. Now the principal has agreed for them not to take part in the drills, if only they do not obstruct the others. By this time the drills have become a farce and are so treated by teachers who do not mark down the names of delinquents. There has been a change of the rules, not against the dissenters but for them.

Our Unitarians, etc., are balked also by their false Realism and Practicality. They remain in a framework of action even when it offers no possibilities for *their* kind of action. This occurs at every election. Our friends have an obsessional inability to refrain from marking a ballot, though they are offered no relevant candidates and though their voting confirms the system that has given them the bad candidates. They will not vote for a minor candidate because they do not want to throw away the vote; and they reason that not to vote at all is a futile protest. But the practical alternative is to *actively* not vote, to campaign against voting with an ad in the press and on TV, and picketing one hundred feet from the polls, crying DON'T Vote till we get a candidate representing what we believe. This would, of course, be scandalous—but not so scandalous as having to choose between a Kennedy and a Nixon.

False Practicality is sometimes the bathetic illusion of exerting possible influence if one "works within the system," and naturally the major political parties use window-dressing to attract this kind of support. (Certainly, conceited identification with the powerful works mightily in some of our academics and scientists.) In describing the American Communists of the thirties, Harold Rosenberg has scathingly exposed their lust to be on the governing board no matter what. But in general in America—perhaps because of the methods by which people get office—it is almost out of the question for anybody indignantly to resign; and our intellectuals agree that it would be imprudent for him to give up his chance of exerting influence! But of course his *not* resigning is what exerts a discouraging influence, for it means that no issue is really earnest.

The general class of falsely practical behavior is Choosing the Lesser of Two Evils and there is current an abominable doctrine that *only* such choices indicate that a man is tough-minded and serious, not utopian and dilettantish. (To do them credit, I do not think that the Unitarians, etc., accept this abomination of Dr. Niebuhr and the *New Leader*.) Let us be clear on what is involved here. Choosing the Lesser Evil does not mean accepting half a loaf, or one slice, or even the promise of a crumb tomorrow, but swallowing a milder rat poison rather than a more virulent rat poison. As I have pointed out previously, to be stuck with such a choice means that we have long neglected our duty and interest; there are terrible unfinished situations which prevent the emergence of new possibilities. Then it is to this unfinished business that we must address ourselves, and not choose still another evil to avoid unfinished business. We cannot hope, after long neglect, to escape without suffering. Surely the history of colonialism and its breakdown has taught nothing else but this. Only penitence and magnanimity in making amends can now shorten the time of travail. Gimmicks, gradualism, puppet rulers cannot avail. Since the French must quit Algeria in 1962, it would have helped them to have magnanimously resolved it in 1954. I will merely mention Cuba and South America. But of course the *ne plus ultra* of Choosing the Lesser Evil is accepting Deterrence, even though this policy is likely to produce the maximum calamity, and even though the first stroke of unfinished business in this area would be to call for a national and worldwide mourning for Hiroshima.

False Realism of the better educated is often contempt for plain people and a pessimistic notion of democracy. It is thought that the "mass" of people are not up to ideal or magnanimous behavior; they must be won or pacified in terms of surface prejudices and venal interests; and our real aims must be concealed and debauched by Public Relations. Inevitably such behavior has caused a continual further debasement and confusion of the electorate, so that it is by now almost unknown for an electoral campaign to debate any genuine issue that could be decided by real evidence and real differences of interest. But if there are no real issues, there is no possibility for an inventive or statesman-like resolution of them. Yet the people who must be thus cajoled and tricked are no others than our neighbors who, individually or especially in small groups, are not morons if directly confronted. (In great numbers, to be sure, the whole is less than the summation of its parts.) One of the very few honest public figures whom I know, Congressman Kastenmeier of Wisconsin, has told me that the chief virtue is to be willing to lose; then if one finally wins, one is free and clean. In his opinion, his constituents do not agree with everything he speaks for, but there is mutual respect and they return him.

Finally, our Unitarians, etc., are saddled with their bourgeois and churchly respectability. They are embarrassed, for instance, to give themselves personally to a cause, to carry a sign on the street, rather than sending a telegram or contributing money for an ad. Therefore they do not get the moral and psychological support of solidarity, which comes only from commitment of one's person with one's fellows. Middle-class respectability is squeamish about who its fellows are; it finds it hard to associate with young beards, jeans, and sandals. Nevertheless, it is a mistake for peace actions to discipline themselves to "respectability" in order to win bourgeois support. (Both SANE and the Committee for Non-Violent Action are susceptible to this temptation.) Discipline for such a purpose takes the heart out of any committed behavior, which one must perform as one is, not as one wishes to appear for public relations. Let the others learn that peace is more important than proper clothes. Indeed, one of the most salutary effects of the movements for peace and for civil rights has been just to acquaint respectable people with rough facts; in many a middle-class family these days there has suddenly come to be a member in the common jail or out on bail.

Also it is hard for respectable people to associate themselves with burning but "disreputable" causes. Peace and racial integration are now quite respectable; the repeal of the irrational sex and drug laws is much less so. Yet unfortunately, it is only if the respectable, the professionally competent, and the churches speak up about these laws that we will ever get rid of them.

ii. *Professors and Social Scientists*

In part, well-intentioned and radical professors are kept from decisive action by these same decencies, gullibilities, petty ambitions, and embarrassments. They often have a similar middle-class background of their futility. To be more precise, I think that, as stronger-minded scholars, they are less hampered by moral respectability and mere appearances; but on the other hand, as organization men often working close to the disputed areas, they are more timid about losing their jobs. And as experts, as I have said, they are even peculiarly liable to fall into the trap of being "influential" though they do not determine policy because they are exploited for their brains and not merely as prestigious names. An academic is likely to take enormous pride in seeing his brain-child become great in the world, even as a monster.

Yet the professors are peculiarly puzzling. Their very energy of intellect drives them to make sense, and their ineffectuality is mysterious. Take, roughly as a group, the Committees of Correspondence, writers of newsletters that we circulate to put whatever intellect we have into relaxing the Cold War and preventing the nuclear war. (The ambitious title was chosen to fit the gravity of the task, but it is certainly pompous considering the activity of the members.) Pretty unanimously these correspondents agree that war is not thinkable as a policy; that deterrence is suicidal; that the garrison state is undermining liberty and morality; that the American administration is not bona fide in its peace talk—does nothing to reconvert the economy, it lies to us, etc.; and indeed that national sovereignty must go. Nevertheless, whenever there is an actual event—a "crisis" in Berlin, a resumption of testing—at once the professors start over as if they had not made up their minds, and they bat it around in the terms of the front page of the *Times*. They argue the technical pros and cons; they sympathize with Jack Kennedy's difficulties; they advise the government. They even go so far as to indulge in the speculations of war-game theory, their difference from the Rand Corporation being that the Rand people want to win whereas our people prove that we must lose. In the New York Committee, of which I am a laggard member, the watchword is research. This means research not on how to make our wishes prevail, but on the inaccuracies of Herman Kahn!

Of course, professors are academics and suffer the moral hazards of that situation, the disconnection of thought and practice, the checkrein of administrators who make the important decisions, immurement with adolescents whom they can neither lead nor mix with, the vanity of classroom authority and battles of book reviews. Also there is little community of the faculty in American universities, and we suffer from the disastrous German rule of "academic freedom" that forbids faculty pronouncements in politics. As we have it in America, the academic environment is not calculated to produce commitment and engagement as a climax of intellectual conviction. (Under other circumstances, of course, academic society has been admirably apt for intellectual engagement.) Just as in their schools, where Administration sets up the syllabus and the classes, the professors seem to require somebody else's framework in order to act; they can think and criticize, they cannot initiate policy out of their own convictions. They demonstrate that the official position will ruin us, but they panic at any unofficial alternative.

Yet the pathology goes deeper than this environmental conditioning. There is a political pathology in the essence of contemporary social theory that makes revolutionary alternatives inconceivable to the social scientists. With the best will in the world they cannot see any source of power outside the established power, so there is no point in wishing or talking in other terms, even though the established power has no other *raison d'être* than to wage the Cold War! The social scientists are balked by the narrowness of what they regard as admissible evidence. Contemporary social theory consists in analyzing the arrangement and possible rearrangement of units that are defined as entirely socialized to the system of society, or as deviant. The theory omits animal nature, which cannot be entirely socialized; it omits history, which tells us that men have been very different from those they are dealing with; it omits political philosophy, which tells what men ought to be if life is to be worth living; it omits poetic literature, which imagines other ways of being men. But if we omit these approaches and deal only with "men as they are," we are soon left with the world of the front page and of TV, as if this were the real world. In that world there is no other power than the established power, of force, publicity, status, vested holdings, protocol, and the market. Of these, only the market offers free choices, of course powerfully manipulated; the rest are systematically imposed. On the other hand, there are no conceivable viable alternatives that might newly spring from desire, community, compassion, productive functions, jealous freedom, simple justice, utility, common sense, scholarship, tradition, etc. Such things are hardly mentioned on the front page, but sometimes in obituaries or as human interest.

I have referred above to the merriment that greeted me at Professor Melman's conference on disarmament when I tried to introduce sexual and animal factors as relevant to the discussion of a psychotic system of thought. This mirth was partly, of course, the schoolgirlish embarrassment of professors and statesmen at the mention of copulation; but it was mainly because such factors do not occur, and perhaps cannot occur, in the discussions of the Cold War in the *New York Times* or the *Studies in Deterrence* distributed by Naval Ordnance.

In my opinion, the political pathology of the present social-scientific method is of high importance, so let me give a few random examples of it. Here are some "Psychological Observations on the Student Sit-in Movement," by Drs. Jacob Fishman and Fredric Solomon. The gist is that the Negro sit-ins are a "pro-social acting out," like delinquency acting out deprivation, unconscious parental wishes, aggression and rebellion, but consciously based on moral imperatives, "the goals of conscience representing traditional Christian morality and the highest principles of traditional American democracy." In brief, for these Negro students, "Public action toward social goals is their way of at least temporarily resolving problems of identity, super-ego formation, and aggression." (In like manner, a more assertive behavior of the professors would betoken an unfinished neurotic situation.) In this analysis there is no mention of simple justice, that is, whether traditional Christian morality and American democracy are true or good. There is no mention of human indignation at being insulted, nor of the ingenuous political effort of youth to make a safer and happier world. I doubt that identity can be merely the resolution of an "inner" problem rather than also something to be discovered-and-created, in a community, by a man.

Sometimes the method is almost ludicrous. Criticizing a commodity-oriented suburb, Maurice Stein points out that "The accumulation of appliances can never render cooking permanently meaningful as long as the woman is unsure of its relation to her feminine identity"—and he proceeds to borrow from Erikson the thought that "Identity depends on the accessibility of roles in which acceptance by significant others is assured." True; but oddly, at no point in the discussion does Professor Stein once mention food, feeding, or good cooking, although in the end it must be these that make cooking meaningful and guarantee acceptance, and make the cook proudly feel that she is somebody. It is characteristic of our social scientists never to mention the function, the satisfaction (or danger), the process, the product, or the utility. This leaves out everything in terms of which we could actively *change* anybody's "acceptance" or "rejection." There is no factual criterion outside the system of roles to justify liquidating some of the roles.

Let me give another example along the same lines. In our economic and industrial relations a workman has no say in the utility of the product or the technique of the process; *therefore* his foreground criterion for a job is "security." But under normal conditions, a workman is secure if what he makes is necessary, so that his work is wanted; and if the process employs his aptitudes, so that it is he who is wanted. Yet in management and labor unions both, our social engineers do not think in these terms. Rather, they take the secondary sentiment of "security" as the ultimate desire of the man, and make no effort to cope with the real irk of the job. Men socialized to an unsatisfactory situation are mistaken for "men as they are."

(We utopians are said to want the ideal, which is unrealistic, for society can never provide more than the tolerable. The charge is false. We would be quite content with the tolerable, which would allow individuals to make something of themselves if they have it in them. But it is the way of the present democracy-by-consent to settle for the not-intolerable, for the system to oppress as far as it can without arousing a squawk. Inevitably, as we see in our urbanism, people become inured and resigned to a greater and greater degree of the not-intolerable. Yet none of this will seem important to a sociologist until there is a fantastic explosion.)

In an essay on Vassar, Theodore Newcomb points out that "Students and faculty are two societies occupying the same territory." So Professors Jencks and Riesman on Harvard: "Professors and students know one another as ambassadors from mutually fearful cultures." Pursuing this notion of the colleges "as they are," the social scientists then try to devise a system of education in terms of acculturation of the alien tribes. But by so doing they neglect the possibility of making a good university, one founded on a more correct anthropology, namely that the students and teachers are one society, the students growing up and learning from the teachers as veterans. In the analysis of the professors, the youth subculture is taken as irreducible, whereas the subculture is only their reaction to being balked by adult society. And the teachers are relegated to being forever academics, but it is their embarrassment, timidity, and lack of function in the world that make them so.

Thus, neglecting history, animal and social nature, political philosophy, and poetry, the social scientists are left with a closed society in which nothing is possible but a better arrangement of the same forces. People's opinions, prejudices, neuroses, and fears, as revealed by questionnaires and depth-questionnaires, will fairly reflect the same structure of society—what else would they reflect? But indeed, the questions themselves usually offer only the usual choices. Only the "No Opinion" gets outside the box. Tests of personality are not used for therapy, as they were designed, to open new possibilities for removing personality blocks, but are used precisely for social engineering, to facilitate a more painless and "efficient" adjustment of the same personalities to the same system. Not surprisingly, people increasingly do not adjust —the most recent study says that 80 per cent of persons in midtown Manhattan are nutty—but this is again taken not as a defect in our way of life but as a defect in our way of socializing people to that way of life.

Then suddenly some of the professors notice that the *system as a whole* is drifting toward disaster. The Cold War is "escalating." They cry out in alarm. They underwrite ads in the *Times*. They form Committees of Correspondence. All this is earnest, courageous, nonconforming. But they do not, apparently they cannot, think, or step, outside the framework of the drifting system. The Cold War escalates further; their response does *not* escalate further. They do not say, "I won't." They do not invent.

iii. Practical Syllogism

To explain all this, we must explore further. The professors are balked more by their habits of thought than by their middle-class and academic habits of life. They are intellectuals; inquiry is their existential commitment; if they could habitually think differently, they would eventually live differently. What is the background of their frustrating kind of thought?

The problem can be defined pretty sharply: they reason practically but do not come to the practical conclusion. Consider a practical syllogism of a simple form: "I want an X," "Here is an X," and the conclusion from these premises is *not* another proposition, but an action, to take the X and use it. (So negatively: "This behavior is disadvantageous," "I could stop it," then the conclusion is in fact to stop.) Psychosomatically, the meaning of this simple logic is clear. Where does the energy of action come from? The desire expressed in the first premise is the energy of the action of the conclusion. The second premise is information about the environment that is also selected and attended to because of the desire in the major. And finally, the act, the climax of practical reasoning, is the release to activity of the motoric system that has been held in check during the verbal part. What is this verbal part? Why does the man verbalize his experience at all? Presumably the speaker *says* "I want" as a request or demand of another, and meanwhile holds his own motor behavior in check, waiting for a response. "Here is etc." is seeking orientation: to ascertain the availability, permissibility, location which must be determined for action. Since there is a problem, there is a delay called "thinking"; since there is a useful interpersonal context, there is speech; but the solution of the problem is a feelingful and appropriate action. On the whole, practical reasoning, like any other normal act, is an integration of feeling, sensation, and motor behavior.

In recent models of practical reasoning, however, there is an extraordinary emphasis on a stage called "deciding" or "decision-making." To quote one of the authors, John Corson, "Decision-making is the central and continuing business of every human enterprise." What is implied in this astonishing proposition? Normally, apart from obsessionals, deciding is not a major part of practice.

There is, in the present economic and social arrangements, a high concentration of control of capital, a large (and usually excessive) component of frozen capital regarded as an investment that must pay off, a top-down management of the machinery, long-chain bureaucracy, considerable ignorance and indifference of most workers as to what the enterprise is about, and almost total ignorance of everybody as to what they as persons are about. The style of the products is largely built into the machinery; the style of life into the relations of production; and the style of thought is predetermined by the system itself. Indeed, the limits of choice, of deciding, are narrowly set by what the predetermined thought and style of the system can allow as alternatives. The choice of one or another of the limited alternatives is called "decision-making" and it seems to be vastly important because it "influences" so vast a machine; but of course the influence is slight, because nothing can be decided different from what the machine will accept as a program to operate with. The machine itself cannot be much altered because it is so heavily capitalized and must pay off. And the system of relations as a whole is so tightly controlled and so complicated that it "goes by itself." Little is really decided, but deciding stands out as an act peculiarly potent, important, and free simply because it is so isolated from the matrix of immediate desire, concrete perception, inventive thought, motoric strength and rhythm that constitutes ordinary practical and intellectual life. Managers are prestigious because they are the remnants of men, whereas the others are not men at all.

But the decision-maker, the administrator, is only a remnant. He has little personal desire or concern for the goal; he knows little about the information that comes to him in a form so highly processed that it has often lost the essence of the reality; his act of practical judgment, deciding, is so limited that it expresses little of himself; nor is it he who implements the decision, he does not grow by deciding. In brief, our present style of important practical judgment—corporate, mechanical, managerial—is, psychosomatically, a trivial remnant of normal practice. But it does satisfy the illusory conceit of being a big wheel.

Return now to our professors. My guess is that they, whose private lives are usually pretty restricted, have become so mesmerized by this big style that they no longer remember what it feels like simply to reason and act. Secondarily, they rationalize their avoidance of important life-choices by saying that only "big" decision-making has public consequences. In my opinion, even this rationalization is in error, because normal reasonable practice has great rhetorical force (especially by contrast), whereas corporate, managerial, and public-relations decisions are rightly taken whence they come, as making little significant difference.

(By the way, I do not believe that an advanced technology necessarily involves what I have been describing: concentrated management, bureaucracy, alienation of labor, and the emasculation of practical reasoning to decision-making. Quite the contrary, these are by and large inefficient, unexperimental, uncritical, and discouraging to invention. I write this paragraph because I have learned from experience that to point out structural defects of the present social arrangements is at once to be called a machine-breaker who wants to return to something called the Middle Ages. This is again an example of mesmerized superstition.)

Another important factor in the professors' behavior is their disposition to verbalize experience and keep it verbalized, rather than to use speech as an action upon others. They shun argument *ad hominem*. "Communication" comes to mean the exchange of ideas from one head to another with each person's character defenses left intact and his pattern of behavior unaltered. Speakers put only their formulations at stake, not their lives, their fortunes, or their sacred honor. When they come to share a common idea, it is with the same detachment. Since they have staked nothing and have not committed their persons in their speech, their agreement gives them no strength of solidarity, and there is no engagement in the action that would normally follow on agreement.

This is, of course, what is meant by an argument being academic; since nothing is changed by it, it is always possible to reverse positions and argue the contrary. (It is a good teaching method for the freshman and sophomore years.) Faculty meetings, with their departmental courtesy, are a training-ground: one is supposed to excel in speech in one's field, but it is bad form to insist on anything, for the sake of action, that would invade somebody else's preserve. Scholarly detachment is necessary for intellectual consideration, but finally the flow of words must come home to oneself, in action or character change, otherwise we have mere conversation pieces and ping-pong, a speech-game designed for ceremony, or to show off, or at best to one-up and establish a pecking order.

Effective speech, however, is a personal contact, and the grounds of personal contact, whether affectionate or aggressive, are psychosexual and communal. Until our mores become sexier, dirtier, friendlier, and angrier, we cannot expect intellectual speech to be *ad hominen*. Yet if argument is not at least potentially *ad hominem*, the speaker's lurking motivations and deep-grained habits are never brought into the foreground, challenged, and tested. And without felt motivation and self-awareness of attitude, new reasoning cannot pass into new practice.

To think and then act requires faith. A man must believe that himself and his peers, correcting one another's reasoning and making it common and public, have finally as good a sampling of reality as there is. And they are as adequate judges of it as there are, for any other judgments are merely made by other groups of men who, one has reason to suspect, might be more ignorant or fraudulent. And most important, a man must believe that the world is a world *for* him; if he exercises initiative and takes a step, his action will have an effect, however small, in the same real world. He will not suddenly be without ground underfoot. Faith is animal faith, as Santayana said, but it is also a grounds of poetry, according to philosophy, in the stream of history. It is humane. A man has faith that if he is well intentioned, rational, not fanatical, he is not alone; there is a human community that is thinking the same thoughts as himself and his friends, and ready to act in concert. Of course I do not know where such faith in the nature of things and in the human community comes from, nor how it can be infused. It is faith. It seems to me to be the most proximate cause of initiative. It is not very helpful of me to end these reflections with a confidence that I cannot transfer from my breast to yours. But at least I have tried to show how the conditions of our society discourage it, my hope being that we can then learn to stand out of the way.

April, 1962.

ABOUT THE AUTHOR

Describing himself, PAUL GOODMAN has said, "I am a man of letters in the old sense, one who thinks that the literary process itself, the criticism of life, adds a new and indispensable element." In 1961 Mr. Goodman visited nearly thirty colleges, lecturing in various departments and to student organizations. His chief interest is to find ways to make our environment livable by restoring human scale in modern technological and urban conditions. Accordingly, he has devoted himself also to problems of growth and education. He is a fellow of several associations of psychologists, and has worked especially on problems of career block. He teaches methods of group therapy, and, with Dr. F. S. Perls and Professor Ralph Hefferline, is the author of *Gestalt Therapy*. He has taught at the University of Chicago, New York University, Black Mountain College, and Sarah Lawrence.

Mr. Goodman has written for *Commentary, Politics, Kenyon Review, Dissent, Liberation, Partisan Review*, etc. His books include works of fiction, verse, and social and literary criticism. Among his books in the area of social studies are *Art and Social Nature; Communitas*, a classic work in city planning (written with his brother, Percival, the Professor of Community Planning at Columbia); *Growing Up Absurd*, which received wide attention when it was published in 1960; *Utopian Essays and Practical Proposals;* and *The Community of Scholars* (1962).

Mr. Goodman was born in 1911. He is a graduate of C.C.N.Y. and earned his Ph.D. at the University of Chicago. He is an Associate of the University Seminar on Problems of Interpretation at Columbia. Mr. Goodman, now a resident of New Hampshire, is married and has two children.